Also from Westphalia Press
westphaliapress.org

The Idea of the Digital University Dialogue in the Roman-Greco World

The Politics of Impeachment

International or Local Ownership?: Security Sector Development in Post-Independent Kosovo

Policy Perspectives from Promising New Scholars in Complexity

The Role of Theory in Policy Analysis

ABC of Criminology

Non-Profit Organizations and Disaster

The Idea of Neoliberalism: The Emperor Has Threadbare Contemporary Clothes

Donald J. Trump's Presidency: International Perspectives

Ukraine vs. Russia: Revolution, Democracy and War: Selected Articles and Blogs, 2010-2016

Iran: Who Is Really In Charge?

Stamped: An Anti-Travel Novel

A Strategy for Implementing the Reconciliation Process

Issues in Maritime Cyber Security

A Different Dimension: Reflections on the History of Transpersonal Thought

Contracting, Logistics, Reverse Logistics: The Project, Program and Portfolio Approach

Unworkable Conservatism: Small Government, Freemarkets, and Impracticality

Springfield: The Novel

Lariats and Lassos

Ongoing Issues in Georgian Policy and Public Administration

Growing Inequality: Bridging Complex Systems, Population Health and Health Disparities

Designing, Adapting, Strategizing in Online Education

Secrets & Lies in the United Kingdom: Analysis of Political Corruption

Pacific Hurtgen: The American Army in Northern Luzon, 1945

Natural Gas as an Instrument of Russian State Power

New Frontiers in Criminology

Feeding the Global South

Beijing Express: How to Understand New China

Demand the Impossible: Essays in History as Activism

Unitarian Affirmations: Seven Discourses Given in Washington, D.C.

by Unitarian Ministers

WESTPHALIA PRESS
An imprint of Policy Studies Organization

Unitarian Affirmations: Seven Discourses Given in Washington, D.C.
All Rights Reserved © 2019 by Policy Studies Organization

Westphalia Press
An imprint of Policy Studies Organization
1527 New Hampshire Ave., NW
Washington, D.C. 20036
info@ipsonet.org

ISBN-13: 978-1-63391-810-8
ISBN-10: 1-63391-810-6

Cover design by Jeffrey Barnes:
jbarnesbook.design

Daniel Gutierrez-Sandoval, Executive Director
PSO and Westphalia Press

Updated material and comments on this edition
can be found at the Westphalia Press website:
www.westphaliapress.org

UNITARIAN AFFIRMATIONS:

Seven Discourses

GIVEN IN

WASHINGTON, D.C.

By UNITARIAN MINISTERS.

BOSTON:
AMERICAN UNITARIAN ASSOCIATION.
1890.

Copyright by

AMERICAN UNITARIAN ASSOCIATION.

1879.

THIRD EDITION.

UNIVERSITY PRESS: JOHN WILSON & SON,
CAMBRIDGE.

PREFACE.

THE following seven discourses were delivered on successive Sunday mornings, in the early part of the year 1879, at the new Unitarian Church in Washington City, by invitation of the pastor of the Society and the American Unitarian Association. All except the first were repeated on the same Sunday evenings in the Unitarian Church of Baltimore.

The invitation was that they should be addressed, not especially to scholars and theologians, but to the people.

They were prepared independently of each other; and, for the opinions expressed, the several writers are alone responsible.

BOSTON, May 1, 1879.

CONTENTS.

		PAGE
I.	THE UNIVERSAL AND THE SPECIAL IN CHRISTIANITY	1
	By Rev. Frederic H. Hedge, D.D.	
II.	THE BIBLE	27
	By Rev. James Freeman Clarke, D.D.	
III.	GOD	51
	By Rev. Andrew P. Peabody, D.D.	
IV.	JESUS CHRIST	75
	By Rev. Brooke Herford.	
V.	MAN	107
	By Rev. George W. Briggs, D.D.	
VI.	THE CHURCH: THE SOCIETY WHICH JESUS GATHERED	127
	By Rev. Rufus Ellis, D.D.	
VII.	THE LIFE ETERNAL. — HEAVEN AND HELL	155
	By Rev. Samuel R. Calthrop.	

UNITARIAN AFFIRMATIONS.

I.

THE UNIVERSAL AND THE SPECIAL IN CHRISTIANITY.

BY REV. FREDERIC H. HEDGE, D.D.

"*Then Peter opened his mouth, and said, Of a truth I perceive that God is no respecter of persons; but in every nation he that feareth him and worketh righteousness is accepted with him.*" — ACTS x. 34, 35.

"*Go ye therefore and teach all nations, baptizing them in the name of the Father, and of the Son, and of the Holy Ghost.*" MATT. xxviii. 19.

ST. PETER, if rightly reported in the passage first quoted, exhibits a breadth of view and a spirit of toleration strangely inconsistent with his conduct at Antioch, as witnessed by Paul and condemned by him in his Epistle to the Galatians. There, as we read, he separated himself from the Gentiles, and "walked not uprightly according to the truth of the gospel." Here, on the contrary, as afterward at Jerusalem, he plants himself on Christian ground, and displays a liberality befitting the disciple of him who could see in the Gentile alien a faith not found in Israel.

But, whilst the apostle concedes that true religion and acceptance with God might be found outside of the pale of his own communion, he nevertheless baptizes Cornelius and his household into the fellowship of the Christian Church; thereby implying that Christianity had something to impart that was more and better than any thing that Jew or Gentile could find within the compass of their respective faiths.

Two points are here presented for our consideration: first, that all religions have something in common, — that all agree in their essentials; second, that Christianity has elements peculiar to itself, by virtue of which it ranks superior to other faiths.

All religions have something in common, — all have something divine. The time has gone by when Christianity, in the view of its confessors, could claim a monopoly of saving truth. Recent study of the ethnic religions has abated the contemptuous aversion with which Christian orthodoxy was wont to regard them, waiving them aside as damnable impostures or execrable superstitions, and their receivers as without the pale of salvation. This was the view with which Christian missionaries in former time engaged in the noble enterprise of rescuing those lost peoples from their imminent doom by drawing them into the Christian fold. They knew nothing or next to nothing of the religions they wished to supplant; but simply assumed that, not being Christian, they must be utterly and only bad and that all who held them, unless converted and baptized, must perish everlastingly. If any one maintain that such a conviction alone can inspire the zeal required for missionary effort I reply that zeal without insight — that is, without truth — can never produce the best fruits of the Spirit. The most it can accomplish is a formal confession induced by fear. Its converts will be the least enlightened and least honorable among the people addressed. One cannot but respect the temper of the Norseman who was willing to be baptized, but when the missionary represented the alternative as everlasting damnation, and, in answer to his questioning, assured him that all his ancestors, not having heard of the gospel, were in that predicament, withdrew his foot from the water, preferring rather to be damned with his fathers than saved without them. If the missionary had but known it, there was more of Christianity and more of salvation in that reply than in all the dogmas of his creed and all the sacraments of his Church.

Of course, the missionary must believe in the superiority of his own religion. Without that belief, no missionary is qualified, or is likely to undertake, its promulgation in heathen lands. But this conviction does not necessarily imply indiscriminate, unqualified condemnation of other religions as wholly and only false and bad. The best-prepared missionary is he who adds to zeal and purity of purpose a knowledge of the mental condition, the way of thinking, the ideas and beliefs of those whom he seeks to convert, a disposition to learn, and the feeling that it is his business to learn, as well as to teach, that one important end of his mission is to gain new light for the illustration of the gospel from other dispensations. The missionaries who have wrought in this spirit have done a good work by faithful use of their opportunities in acquiring and importing into Christendom a knowledge of the faith and ideas of Gentile lands. Such knowledge enables the Christian to operate with surer method and better effect on the nations so reported. Our acquaintance with the Oriental religions is chiefly derived from the labors of such men as Wilson, Spence Hardy, Ellis, and the Abbé Huc. Our best knowledge of the works of Confucius, founder of the eldest religion of China, we owe to Dr. Legge of the London Missionary Society, "who gives it as the result of twenty-one years of missionary experience that he could not consider himself qualified for the duties of his position until he had thoroughly mastered the classical books of the Chinese, and investigated for himself the whole field of thought through which the sages of China had ranged and which gave the foundation of the moral, social, and political life of the people."* Not till then did he feel himself to be in a condition to preach Christianity to the Chinese.

Above all, it is required of the missionary that he respect the faith of the people to whom he ministers, and frankly recognize whatever in it is worthy and true. "Every religion," says Max Müller, "even the most imperfect and degraded, has something that ought to be sacred to us. There is in all religions a secret yearning after the true though unknown God. Whether we see the Papua squatting in dumb meditation before his fetish, or whether we listen to Ferdusi

* Quoted from Max Müller.

exclaiming, 'The height and depth of the whole world have their centre in thee, O my God; I know not what thou art, but I know that thou art what thou alone canst be,'—we ought to feel that the ground whereon we stand is holy."

All religions have something in them of divine import. However poor, earthly, unspiritual, monstrous even, the materials, the doctrine, and the rite that compose their service, they are kindled from above. The altar may be fed with base superstitions, with cruelty and pain, with self-torture and human sacrifice; but no altar could ever burn until a spark of heavenly fire, a ray from the everlasting God, had descended upon it. The uses may be false and detestable, but the purpose is true and the end is holy. Adoration, Purification, Reconciliation,—these are the purpose and the end, whatever name the religion may bear, whatever methods employ, whatever phase it may assume.

Common to all religions is the belief in Godhead. Infinitely various are the creeds which express this fundamental belief, infinitely various the systems which formulate it and in which it subsists,—monotheism in one race, polytheism in another; Trinitarianism in this church, Unitarianism in that; but what lies at the core of these various systems is substantially the same, — belief in superhuman, absolute Power.

There is one apparent exception to this universality, and that in the case of the religion which numbers at present the largest following, — a following in all its branches of more than four hundred millions of believers, — the religion of Buddhism. But even here the exception is only partial: it relates to some of the attributes of Deity, not to the essential fact. The Buddhist has no God in the sense of an aboriginal, supermundane Power, creator, and ruler of the universe: he believes that the universe is a power in itself, self-existent, eternal. But the Buddhist adores the founder of his faith, the king's son who renounced his inheritance, who made himself poor, of no account, and by faith and patience overcame the world and attained to perfection of holiness. The Buddhist makes a God of him, and worships in him the superhuman ideal, the infinite greatness and worth.

In one or another form, with different names, with endless modifications, every religion holds the fundamental article of Godhead. Every religion offers something superhuman to believe in, to restrain, to aspire after, to adore. If it be but a shapeless block, that block represents the supernal and divine to the cowering savage who prostrates himself before it in prayer. In this primary article all religions agree; and let us add, they are all in this alike imperfect. Paul found the Athenians worshipping an unknown god. Is not this the condition of worshipping humanity the world over, even now? Is not all religion a feeling after God, if haply we may find Him who is never far from any one of us, and whose very nearness perhaps conceals him? Who knows God except in those points of osculation in which our limited nature touches his? What sage or saint who has spent his life in devout contemplation can say, "I know him quite." What religion, the purest and most enlightened, presents him otherwise than in part? Who that is truly and wisely devout will not confess with Fichte: "I veil my face before thee and lay my hand upon my mouth. How thou art in thyself, how thou appearest to thyself, I can never know, so surely as I never can be thou. After thousand times thousand spirit-lives lived through, I shall no more be able to comprehend thee than in this earthly hut. That which I comprehend becomes by my comprehending it finite, and the finite can never by any process of magnifying and exalting become infinite."

SPECIAL IN CHRISTIANITY. 9

Common to all religions and fundamental in all is the notion of duty, the feeling of moral obligation, with its correlate, moral accountability. Every religion, savage or civilized, whatever else it might teach or fail to teach, has said to its votaries, "Thou shalt," and "Thou shalt not." They command and forbid. The commandments and prohibitions are not the same in all: they vary indefinitely. The specifications of right and wrong, the applications of the moral law, differ widely in different systems; but the idea of law, the sense of right and wrong, requirement and prohibition, are in all. So rooted in human nature is the feeling of duty, that man instinctively fetches his commandments from a source above himself until he has learned the meaning of right, and has come to feel the absolute authority of what is meant by that term. Until then, he derives the obligation of the law from arbitrary command; that is, he puts power before right, makes power the source and measure of right, and conceives that right is right only because commanded, and not rather commanded because right. Thus religion becomes the moral educator of mankind. By positive precept and external authority, it trains the yet undeveloped moral sense until man learns to find the law and the reason of the law in himself, and by the light of his own perceptions to choose the good and avoid the evil.

Say not that religion is degraded by making it subservient to the moral nature, instead of an independent and the supreme interest in life. There is nothing higher in man than righteousness. That is the top of being; and religion fulfils its best function, though by no means its only function, when it aids our ascent to that supreme height. Nay, more: the truth of its moral ideas is the standard by which every positive religion must be judged. A form of religion, a scheme of doctrine, which affronts or fails to satisfy our sense of right, carries with it its own condemnation.

There is one thing more which all religions have in common, — the promise of a better hereafter, the hope of redemption, release from the burden and the trial, the weary struggle, the pains and discontents of mortal life; — Heaven, which different systems figure with very different conditions, according to the habits and culture of their receivers, but which all agree in representing as a state of painlessness and rest. *Heaven*, I say, not *Immortality*. Immortality is an after-thought, a metaphysical abstraction which supervenes, not the primary, the essential element in the universal hope. And in one of the religions already referred to it is doubtful if immortal life, or life at all, in our sense of the term, can be predicated of that hope. Buddhism differs from other religions in divesting the final Rest of those attributes of conscious thought and will without which the Western mind can conceive of no heaven. The Buddhist heaven is a state of actionless, aimless, will-less repose, — Nirvana; concerning which it is a question with the critics whether to regard it as a form of existence at all, or not rather as cessation of individual life. Be that as it may, to the Buddhist, in whose estimation existence as such is an evil, Nirvana is an object of desire, a wished-for goal, a supreme hope. And in that sense Buddhism has also, like the other religions, a heaven in its creed.

God, duty, heaven; worship, obedience, hope, — these are constituents in every religion. And this consent of all faiths in what is most essential bears significant witness of the common mind of which all races and nations, in their several degrees of capacity and culture, partake. Thus, in all religions there is something saving and divine. When the apostle says, "By faith are ye saved," it is not the topics of faith but the faculty of faith that possesses this saving power.

Admire with me this faculty of faith, that heavenly spark which the Everlasting has lodged in the human breast, by which man can overtop himself and overcome the world, can glory in tribulation, walk through fire, condemn himself to life-long torture, and find repose on the rack; can record his thought in scriptures that shall live when the language in which they are written has ceased for a thousand years to be spoken by living men, for which colleges shall be founded and which men of genius shall spend their lives in deciphering, — that faith that can express its convictions in mountains of stone which Nature shall adopt as her own, granting them, as the poet says, "an equal date with Andes and with Ararat."

We have now to inquire what the Christian religion adds to these fundamentals; what special and characteristic features distinguish it from, and exalt it above, the other religions of the world.

It has been the custom of Christian apologists, when contrasting their own with other dispensations, to rest the superiority of the former on the ground of its moral code. Christianity, they have claimed, excels all other religions as a practical rule of life. I very much question the validity of this argument. To substantiate the alleged superiority of the Christian dispensation in this particular, it needs not only be shown that certain precepts of the gospel are peculiar, and surpass the moral import of other codes, — a point, by the way, which those who are best acquainted with the sacred books of other religions will be least inclined to insist on, — but also it must be shown that those precepts have fructified in the life; that Christians in the mass are morally better than the subjects of other faiths. For what does it signify that Jesus as a moralist contemplated a higher standard than Confucius or Gautama or Zoroaster, if the Christian Church has failed to realize that standard in the peoples subject to its sway? If this criterion be applied, it is far from certain that the claim of moral superiority can be established. It is doubtful if Christian nations are better than others, except so far as intellectual progress — *which is not the product of religion, but of race and clime* — has raised the moral standard in lands the most advanced, intellectually and politically, of those that bear the Christian name.

Compare the average Christian of the Eastern Church in Syria or Asia Minor with the average Turk or Jew, his neighbor: I doubt if the comparison will much redound to the advantage of the former. It is also to be observed, in this connection, that Jesus did not claim for his moral system any thing more than the fulfilment of the Hebrew code.

It is not in its ethics that I find the true distinction of the Christian dispensation, but in its theory, its far-reaching and reconciling vision, its humanitarian scope and intent.

Characteristic of Christianity is its intimate, organic relation to its founder. This seems to be symbolized in its very name. All historic religions are designated by the names of their authors by those outside of their pale; but within their several folds they have other appellations. Christianity is so designated, not only by outsiders, but by its disciples. The religion has no other name, or — if the use of the word "gospel" be thought a limitation of this assertion — none so universal as this. The fact is significant: it shows that the consciousness of Christendom connects the religion indivisibly with its author, as being not merely a teacher of certain truths which can be detached from the teacher, and which, provided they are received, it matters not whence they are derived, but as being, in a sense, himself the religion taught; a principle implanted, a power embodied, in the Christian Church, which constitutes the life of its life, and which no analysis less searching than the supreme chemistry of death can eradicate thence. Suppose we had the precise teachings of Jesus without his personality, — a doctrine derived from an unknown source or referred to some venerable name like that of Pythagoras or Plato; and suppose a body of followers organized for the maintenance and practice of that doctrine, — would that be essential Christianity, — Christianity in all but the name? It would be so perhaps from the point of view of what is called Free Religion, but not as the Christian world understands Christianity. Christianity, as the Christian world receives it, is the doctrine of Jesus *plus* the personality. That personality is a spiritual force introduced into human society, which lives and works in the world to this day. The same is true in a measure of every great personality. Every great and noble life once lived in the world becomes a part of the world for evermore. To find the distinctive in Christianity, therefore, we have further to inquire what it is that the personality of Jesus represents, as distinguished from other wise and holy men, — teachers, prophets, founders of new faiths. The answer is given in the phrase, "Son of God," an epithet applied to no other teacher in the sense in which it is applied to him and appropriated by him.

Jesus represents divine Sonship. I say *represents:* that word implies something behind the representative, an antecedent idea or fact. The representation includes the being, illustrates it by a special example, but does not bound it, does not confine it, does not exhaust it. Divine sonship is not exhausted by Christ. It is no monopoly conferred by birth or purchased by blood. Paul says grandly, "As many as are led by the spirit of God are sons of God." "Partakers of the divine nature," says the Second Epistle of Peter. *Humanity* is the son of God, Humanity in *esse* or in *posse*. This is the truth which Jesus represents, which he illustrates by a supreme instance.

We have here, then, a distinguishing feature of the Christian dispensation: it reveals a divine sonship, implying as its correlate the fatherhood of God.

And that fatherhood of God, in the sense in which the gospel presents it, is also a peculiarity of the Christian faith. Not that the appellative Father, as applied to God, is wanting in other religions, Jewish and Gentile; but in them it signifies, as I understand it, fatherly care, not identity of essence, — not the *homousian* affinity of God with man which Jesus intends when he says, " I and the Father are one," and which he recognizes in his followers, — " As thou, Father, art in me, and I in thee, that they may be one in us." If the text seem to limit this affinity to Christian believers, we are to understand that limitation as strictly subjective, — a limitation of consciousness, not of nature. Christianity affirms an affinity, an essential unity of God and man, — a divinity in man, a humanity in God; a divine humanity unknown in other religions, distinguishing it from Jewish and Mohammedan monotheism on the one hand, and Hellenic polytheism on the other. The God of Judaism is a sharply defined individual, high and lone, between whom and man there was no communication but through the ministry of angels, or mediating voices speaking " to the fathers by the prophets." On the other hand, the Græco-Italic theology (and the same is true of the Indian and Egyptian) presented a multitudinous host of questionable individualities, deifications of nature, or deified men, a confused tissue of "genealogies and old wives' fables," in which the central Unity was lost, and whose mythic immoralities ignored the supreme Holiness. Christianity is the reconciliation and corrective of these extremes. It preserves the essential unity of Semitic monotheism without its rigidity and insulation. It preserves the expansiveness and inclusiveness of ethnic polytheism without its dissolutions and corruptions. The God of Christianity is one, but not an individual; undivided and uncircumscribed; unity, but not a unit; not spatially secluded and self-confined like the Hebrew Jehovah, but space-pervading and self-imparting, equally removed from egoistic isolation on one side and indiscriminate monism on the other; not the impersonal God of a levelling pantheism, which knows but one agent as well as one substance, yet not a fixed, reserved, but an ever-proceeding personality.

This leads me to speak of another distinguishing feature of the Christian dispensation. This flowing personality is what is meant by the Holy Spirit. Proper to Christendom is the confession of the Holy Spirit. I do not assert that no trace of belief in spirit can be found outside of the Christian world. I cannot forget those memorable words of Seneca: "There is a holy spirit within us, observer of our good and our evil; our guardian who treats us according as he is treated by us." But the spirit intended by Seneca was an individual spirit, a good genius. The affirmation of the Spirit as a fundamental article of theology, as a necessary element in the concept of Godhead, is peculiar to Christianity. No other religion before or since has ever proclaimed that quickening, energizing truth. The writers of the New Testament did not undertake to define it, they delivered no dogma concerning it: they simply affirmed it as one of the aspects and modes of Deity, a member of that divine "Economy" in the faith of which Christian converts were to be baptized. But the theologians of other centuries reasoned and wrangled about it until it well-nigh vanished from the Church, until the virtue and the power of it were lost in a formula. That formula, intended to be final, was indorsed with a codicil which rent Christendom asunder. We need not perplex ourselves with the question whether, as held by the Eastern Church, the Spirit proceeds from the Father alone, or whether, as affirmed by the Western, it proceeds from the Father and the Son: enough that it proceeds,—eternally proceeds. Think of it, dwell on it, ponder the intense significance of that idea! — Spirit not an entity, not a fixed quantum, but a process, a process for ever renewed, a flowing personality, Godhead in flux. What other religion has propounded an idea so deep-searching, so far-reaching, so all-embracing? By participation of the Spirit, and in the degree in which man is penetrated, possessed, and renewed by the Spirit, he is one with God, the son with the Father. For only of the spiritual man is the saying true, — only he, in the plenitude of his God-consciousness, will dare to appropriate it, — "I and the Father are one." Not man as member of the animal kingdom, — not man, the head of the anthropoids, — but he whom Paul terms "the second man," "the Lord from heaven;" the man whom no law of nature has fetched from original protoplasm, whom no doctrine of evolution can derive from ancestral *monéra*, though billions of years be allowed for the process.

Father, Son, and Spirit, — we have here the characteristic confession of the Christian faith. But is not this the old ecclesiastical tradition which the very name of our communion, the name Unitarian, is understood to repudiate? Why not say "Trinity" at once, and so confess the Unitarian protest to have been a mistake? For sundry sufficient reasons. I am speaking of what is peculiar to Christianity; but Trinity is found in other religions,— notably in the well-known instance of the Indian *trimurti*, a dogma of the Brahman. Then, the word " Trinity" is misleading. It brings into theology a numerical element; it changes the question of Godhead from an ontological to a numerical one; and, in spite of all apologies and protests, it points in the direction of tritheism. There is no mention of trinity in the New Testament, none in the Christian writers of the first century. In an evil hour, Tertullian, in his controversy with Praxeas, toward the close of the second century, made use of the word *trinitas*, and with it unwittingly flung an apple of discord into the Church, over which theologians have agonized and clamored and wrangled from then until now. Questions arose, of substance and hypostasis, of *homousion* and *homoiousion*, *monothelete* and *dyothelete*, which had as little to do, I will not say with practical Christianity, but with Christian theology as presented in the New Testament, as the incarnations of Vishnu.

Beside its irrelevancy and perversion of essential Christianity, I furthermore object to the doctrine of the Trinity its inadequacy. It assumes to be a complete statement of the substance, or, if you will, of the personality of God; but it takes no note of Nature, — the all-present manifestation of God, — and compels the alternative, either to set aside Nature as Godless, or accept her as an independent God.

The Unitarian reform was a needful protest against the confusion and polytheistic leaning of Trinitarian theology. But if Unitarianism were understood to deny the doctrine of Father, Son, and Spirit, or even to waive and ignore it as unessential, then should I repudiate the name, renounce the connection, and desire that my name were expunged from the muster-roll of that communion. For this is of the very essence of Christianity; and not only so, but indispensable to any right and worthy conception of Deity. Not an abstruse speculation is it, but a vital element of Christian experience.

Other teachings of the gospel have been claimed as peculiar to the Christian dispensation. Some, I think, — and notably the doctrine of grace, as enunciated by Paul, — may be fairly so regarded. But I know of none so distinctive, so constitutive as those which I have named, none of which it is so certain that they have no parallel in other systems. I emphasize, then, this supreme idiom of our religion, — Father, Son, and Spirit. Into this the Christian ages from of old have been baptized; in this name we all, as many of us as have received Christian baptism, have been united to the Church. In this confession the two great divisions of the Christian world, the Eastern and the Western, meet; in this the various Protestant communions are one. The dogma of the Trinity confuses and divides, but this is common, this universal. In words which I have used elsewhere and here beg leave to repeat: "The belief in the Father, the Son, and the Holy Spirit embraces and œcumenizes Christendom in one household of faith. We have in this tenet a God whose nature is neither diffracted by multiplicity nor yet concluded in singularity, who is neither the indifferent All of Pantheism nor the insulated Self of Judaism; a God whose essence is not to be sought in lone seclusion, but in everlasting self-communication; whose being is one and yet a process; a constant reflection of himself in human nature; a ceaseless inchurching of himself in human society."[*]

[*] See "Christian Examiner" for March, 1860.

Christianity, as now presented, is universal religion *plus* the doctrine of Father, Son, and Spirit. That doctrine, while it marks a distinction between the gospel and other systems, is not limitation, but enlargement of the ground which is common to all. It extends the horizon of religious thought, and is therefore an essential of free religion. For free religion does not consist in ecclesiastical indifference, or heterogeneous association of differing creeds, or in bold negations, but in breadth of view.

Comparative religion is the order of the day; but let Christians, or inheritors of the Christian faith, who compare the systems and creeds of nations, beware lest, in their tenderness for other religions, in their anxiety to give those religions their due they fail to do justice to their own. Christians may or may not be better in the main than the subjects of other dispensations; but, to him who rightly apprehends the scope of the gospel, there is in it that which, in height and breadth and depth, as far transcends the wisdom of other faiths as theirs transcends the wild idolatries which they displaced. That was a brave saying of Peter, that "God is no respecter of persons, but in every nation he that feareth him and worketh righteousness is accepted of him." Nevertheless, it needs to be added that, in quite a new and peculiar sense, "grace and truth came by Jesus Christ."

II.

THE BIBLE.

BY REV. JAMES FREEMAN CLARKE, D.D.

"Who also hath made us able ministers of the new testament, not of the letter, but of the spirit; for the letter killeth, but the spirit giveth life." — 2 CORINTHIANS iii. 6.

I AM to speak to you to-day of the Bible, and I propose to describe and contrast the old and new views of the Bible. I shall try to show you that the free, broad, and human views of the Bible long held by Unitarians are now largely accepted by scholars and thinkers of all denominations. I would also show that they are higher, nobler, more spiritual, more religious, than the old Orthodoxy. But before doing this, I will state the facts concerning the Bible in which all agree, — to which all scholars, whether Trinitarians or Unitarians, Orthodox or Heterodox, would assent.

All, then, agree that the Bible is not *one* book, written at one time, and on one subject; but a whole encyclopædia of religious literature. These books were written by at least forty different authors, and during a period of at least a thousand years. By whom they were first gathered together we do not know. At what time they came together we cannot tell. On what principle they were selected is a matter of conjecture. Who the real writers were is doubtful. Their manuscripts have long since perished. The oldest manuscript we have is three hundred years later than the time when the last book of the New Testament was written. Down to the time of the invention of printing, in the fifteenth century, the books of the Bible were copied by hand. The result was that a large number of errors crept in, and we have no means of deciding with certainty what the original text of the Bible was. Our present English version was made by order of King James I., and printed in 1611. Neither the translators were inspired, nor the printers, nor the proof-readers; nor did they possess as good a Hebrew and Greek text from which to translate as we have now.

These are simple matters of fact, to which all scholars will agree, no matter how orthodox they are. On the other hand, all — even the most heretical — whose opinions deserve any respect, will admit that the collection of Jewish

and Christian works which we call the Bible
stands at the head of the religious literature of
the world. There is no book like it, or second
to it. All the other sacred books of mankind, —
the Vedas, the Kings, the Zend Avesta, the writings of Confucius, the Koran, the Eddas, — however much they may contain of sound truth and
moral beauty, are flat and tame when compared
to the depth, sweep, variety, picturesque character,
and heavenly charm of the books of the Bible.
The book of Job is probably the noblest poem in
any literature; the book of Ruth, by the testimony of such critics as Rousseau and Goethe, is
the tenderest idyl; the book of Ecclesiastes is
more terrible in its desperate despair than any
tragedy of Æschylus or Shakspeare. The stories
of patriarchal life in Genesis, and of antique manners in the books of Kings, surpass even the undying charm of those in Herodotus. The book
of Psalms goes so deeply into the spiritual experiences of man's nature — his faith, his doubt, his
reason, his hope, his tender trust, his ardent aspiration — that it will always remain the best
manual of devotion for the human race. The
prophetic literature of the Bible stands absolutely
alone, making a class by itself in the productions
of human genius. Those strains mount up into

the sky like the larks on the plains of Normandy, who ascend higher and higher till they go out of sight in the heavens, while their notes still fill the air with music dropping from above. The writings of Paul contain occasional bursts of fiery eloquence, of tender affection, of concentrated thought, without a parallel in human writings. And the words of Jesus, preserved in the four Gospels, stand for ever alone. For in them we see a harmony of qualities everywhere else separate and divorced. They show us a reformer free to the verge of radicalism, yet a conservative unwilling that a jot of the old law should pass away until the good in it had been carried up to something better; a philanthropist, in whose mind all barriers between man and man had fallen away; — one with a zeal so determined that he went directly to death as a martyr to the truth; and with a charity so large that it included in its embrace all who wished to do the will of his Father in Heaven, however sunk in misery, sin, and shame; a piety so high and so constant that it enabled him to say what no other saint or sage could ever dare to utter, "I and my Father are one." And all these powers of soul, heart, mind, are in such perfect harmony that not one of them is prominent, and that we never think of Jesus as reformer, philanthropist, saint, or martyr, but only as a divinely pure brother, teacher, and friend. Even the Roman Catholic Church has, we think, never ventured to say " Saint Jesus."

The book which contains all this, and vastly more, is justly called " The Bible," or " The Book." There are two diametrically opposite views, however, taken of its origin, inspiration, and authority. One of these I call the theology of the spirit, and the other that of the letter.

The theology of the letter says of the Bible that it is " the word of God " in such a sense that every part of it proceeded by direct revelation from God. It is a supernatural revelation of God's truth, containing every thing necessary for the religious life of man; for his happiness here, and his hope hereafter. The writers were supernaturally and miraculously inspired, so that they could not make any mistake, and have not made any. There are no errors and no contradictions in the Bible. It is infallibly, verbally, literally true from end to end. All between its lids is the word of God. Its geology, astronomy, chronology, are perfect, and leave nothing to be desired. Its great men are all saints to be admired and imitated, their crimes excused and explained away. Its Jewish part and its Christian part are in exact and entire harmony; and he who questions or denies any thing in it is an infidel, who had better have never been born.

This view of the infallibility of the letter of the Bible, — or, as it was once called, its "plenary inspiration," — is not so very ancient, after all. It came up, in its extreme form, since the Reformation. Tholuck, the German theologian, a scholar highly esteemed in all orthodox circles, tells us, in his essay on Inspiration, that this doctrine arose in the controversy with the Roman Church. The Jesuits said, "We, in our church, have unity, confidence, assurance. We have an outward infallible church to lean upon, — an outward authority to which all can appeal, an outward judge to decide all questions. You Protestants have no such authority; nothing infallible, nothing sure. You have only your own inward emotions, different opinions, changing moods." Pressed by this argument, says Tholuck, the Protestants came, by degrees, to maintain that they also had an outward infallible authority, namely, the infallible letter of the Bible; and at last were driven, by the heat of controversy, to assert that not only the sense of the Bible, but the words, the letters, the Hebrew vowel-points, and the very punctuation, proceeded

THE BIBLE. 33

directly from God; and that the writers of the Bible were merely the amanuenses of the Holy Spirit, — the pen with which he wrote, the flute through which he breathed.

Now I will call your attention to the fact that the writers of the Bible lay no claim to any such infallibility as this. They nowhere say that they were inspired to write books. Luke, for instance, gives his reason for writing his Gospel. He does not even say, like a modern Spiritualist, that "he wrote under influence," or that "his hand began to write by an irresistible power." He virtually says, just as you or I might say in the dedication to the biography of a friend, "Forasmuch as many have taken in hand to set forth in order a declaration of those things which are most surely believed among us, even as *they* (who were eye-witnesses and servants of the word from the beginning) delivered them unto us, it seemed good to me, also, having had perfect understanding of all things from the very first, to write unto thee, in order, most excellent Theophilus, that thou mightest know the certainty of those things wherein thou hast been instructed." If Luke were conscious of being divinely inspired to write an infallible book, would he have given such reasons as he does here? He does not say, "You may be certain of the truth of what I say because I am infallibly inspired to write;" but, "You may be sure of the truth of what I say because I have known all about it from the beginning; because I heard it from those who were eye-witnesses; and so I thought it well to write this narrative."

Two texts are quoted to prove this verbal inspiration; and, because thus perpetually quoted, we may presume that they are the strongest which can be found. One says that "Holy men of old spake as they were moved by the Holy Spirit." But it does not say that this made them infallible. Holy men *now* declare that they are moved by the Holy Spirit; but they do not profess to be infallible. The other text says that "All scripture is given by inspiration, and is profitable for doctrine, instruction, &c." Yes, profitable or useful; but that is surely not the same thing as infallible authority. These texts teach an inspiration which I also gladly accept; they do not limit inspiration to the Jews or to the Bible; they teach that all holy men and all sacred books come from God, and have more or less of his truth and power and goodness in them. Yes, " all scripture *is* given by inspiration;" the scriptures of every race and every land; every sacred book which has tamed man's pride, taught him to look up and adore, instructed him to be just, humane, true, and generous. No such books come wholly from the will of man; there is a divine element in them all, whether they are the Vedas of India, or the Koran, or the Dialogues of Plato, or Wordsworth's Ode to Immortality. For "Every good gift and perfect gift is from above, and cometh down from the Father of lights."

There are many serious objections to this doctrine of the infallible inspiration of the Bible, some of which I will now mention.

To say that every statement in the Bible comes directly from God produces widespread unbelief. A large part of the scepticism and infidelity of the present time may be traced directly to this source. Men are taught, from a thousand pulpits, that they are not Christians unless they believe the Bible all true, from Genesis to Revelation. But they cannot believe this, therefore they think they are not Christians. The Bible says that the world was created in six days; that by the genealogies from Adam to Abraham, and Abraham to Christ, it was created less than six thousand years ago; that the sun, moon, and stars were all created at that time; that the visible universe, as well as the human race, has, therefore, existed only during that period. But geology shows us, by infallible documents, written on tables of stone, that the life of the earth, with that of innumerable plants and animals, goes back for millions of years; and astronomy proves that the light which we receive to-day from some distant stars left them hundreds of thousands of years ago. Anthropology shows us, by human bones and stone implements found in ancient strata, that man must have existed in long distant periods of time, far beyond the epoch ascribed to the creation of Adam.

Now, when men are told that they must renounce the revelations of science and the truths of history, or they cannot be Christians, some will make, reluctantly, that sad renunciation. They will abdicate reason, put a bandage over their eyes, and refuse to see facts, and call this voluntary blindness faith. Others will, I think more nobly, prefer to be called infidels rather than to tell a lie for God, or profess to believe what they know to be false. I have had persons tell me that they were infidels because they could not believe that the whale swallowed Jonah, or that Joshua made the sun stand still. I assured them that in order to believe in Jesus Christ it was not necessary to believe in Jonah, or to have any opinions in regard to Joshua. Students of the Old and New Testament find many contradictions between different books. Look at any harmony of the four Gospels, and you will find the same story told differently by the different Evangelists. These contradictions are of no consequence at all; do not diminish our confidence in the truth of the narrative; rather increase our sense of the honesty of the narrators; unless we adopt this theory of the infallibility of the record, and then they become fatal. They differ in details, as human testimony will, but they agree in essentials.

No one can tell how much misery has been caused in honest minds by this old doctrine of scripture infallibility. Some people are made with that sense of truth that they cannot shut their eyes to plain facts because they wish to; cannot make themselves believe by pure will. They reverence the character and teachings of Jesus, and would gladly become his disciples, but do not dare to do so because they cannot accept as true what their reason tells them is false. To such as these the doctrine of the Bible which I am presently to unfold brings hope and healing.

How many superstitions and cruelties have

been sanctified by appeals to the letter of the Scriptures! During many centuries, thousands of poor wretches were burned alive as witches, and this belief rested on the universal conviction of Catholics and Protestants that the Bible clearly taught the reality of witchcraft. A single bishop caused six hundred to be burned. A French judge, Remy, boasted that he had burned eight hundred witches. A thousand persons were executed for this offence in one year in the province of Como, in Italy. Catholic bishops and Protestant clergymen led the way. Luther said, "I would have no compassion on witches. I would burn them all." And all these horrors were triumphantly defended by the letter of the Bible.

So, in our day, we have seen slavery defended, and despotism defended, by the letter of the Bible. Because Paul said, "Slaves, obey your masters," and "The powers that be are ordained of God," it was thought that God commanded men by Paul to submit to a despot like Nero, and ordered them to support a system which made of human beings chattels. So, too, to-day, single words of the Bible are quoted to defend the doctrine that God has made creatures certain to fall into sin, and then punishes them for that

THE BIBLE. 39

sin with endless torments. Such are the superstitions, dishonorable to God, and bringing untold miseries on man, which have been maintained in the world by this view of the Scriptures.

It has also brought about a confusion of Judaism and Christianity. The Old Testament, in some minds, has more authority than the New. In many pulpits Moses has greater influence than Christ. Men still keep the Jewish Sabbath which Christianity abolished. The Lord's day, intended to be a day of freedom and joy, has been made a day of gloom by calling it "the Sabbath," and giving us Moses as our master to teach us what to do in it. Though all that Christ said or did in regard to it was such as to make him a Sabbath-breaker in Jewish eyes, men prefer the law of Moses on this point to his. To rest both the body and soul makes the Christian Sabbath; whatever does that, whether it be a walk, a pleasant conversation, or an entertaining book, is keeping the Sabbath; whatever disturbs the soul with unrest, even if it be church-going, is Sabbath-breaking. The sacrificial worship of the Jews, by which, from morning till evening, the great altar of the Temple ran with blood, has indeed been long abolished. But the influence of that system continues in the Catholic

Church in the daily sacrifice of the Mass, and in the Protestant Church in the blood theology which teaches that God is unable to forgive sin except by bloodshed, and that by the blood of an innocent victim. The Apostles, who were Jews, accustomed to these perpetual sacrifices of the Temple, naturally said, " Christ is our sacrifice." " He is our sin-offering." " It is his blood, not that of goats and sheep, which saves us." And so, literal theology builds on these natural Jewish expressions a whole theory of substituted suffering and vicarious sacrifice.

Thus is the progress of thought arrested; thus is unbelief created; thus are we sent back from Christ to Moses by this Christian literalism. Thus we have a hard and dry theology, which studies the letter, broods over the text, and does not rise to the spirit of the Gospel. To "read the Bible," whether it is understood or not, has been made a Protestant sacrament. Men carry the Bible in their trunk, or keep it on the centre-table as a protecting charm, making the house safer; or, at all events, more respectable. It has been thought dangerous to make any corrections in the text, or the translation, though it is known that there are errors in both.

The chief objection to all this doctrine of the

verbal infallibility of the whole Bible is, that the spirit is chained down by the letter; that the living power of the words and soul of Jesus are neutralized and nullified by being tied to the dead body of old traditions which have long since lost their power. The strength of a chain is only that of its weakest link; so by this doctrine the power of the Bible is kept down to that of its poorest part.

It is a dreadful thing to kill the life of the Gospel by low, literal interpretation. "The letter killeth," says Paul. It does so.

The New Testament teaches, for example, a resurrection of soul and body; but this means ascent, progress, going up into a higher life of soul and a higher life of body. This is animating and inspiring. The New Testament, according to the spirit, shows us perpetual resurrection — endless ascent and progress — heaven above heaven, world above world. It shows us innumerable homes, adapted to all conditions of being; infinite variety there, as there is infinite variety here; of life and joy; of beauty, order, wonder, magnificence; plenty to know, plenty to do, plenty to love. This is our future existence according to the spirit of the New Testament which gives life.

But the theology of the letter tells us, instead, of a resurrection of the same particles of an earthly body; of that flesh and blood which (we are told) cannot inherit the kingdom of God; of that corruptible matter which cannot see incorruption. The letter-theology says that these same poor, sickly bodies are to be gathered out of their graves, and then divided into two classes: one, of saints to go to heaven and sing psalms for ever; the other, of sinners to be sent to hell, there to blaspheme God for ever. Which of these is the most worthy view of the Infinite Being, Creator of all, Father of all, whose sun shines on the evil and good, and whose inexhaustible power and love flow for ever through the universe?

And because of these superstitions we have fierce attacks on the Bible, shallow criticisms on the Bible. When it is made the tyrant instead of the friend, violent reactions come. Some men go about the country denouncing the Bible, filled with an emotional reaction, and quite ignorant of the nobleness, freedom, emancipating power, and broad humanity of this wonderful volume. Others are filled with a critical reaction, and write books to point out an inconsistency here, or a contradiction there, laboring to reduce to a minimum our trust in these grand utterances of the ever-present spirit of God. Because, in their opinion, the Apostle John did not write the fourth Gospel, all its sweet and sacred words are declared to be insignificant.

The theology of the spirit rises above all this level waste of dreary controversy. It regards the Bible as inspired, but not infallible; inspired in a higher degree, by the same spirit which has also spoken to men in all the great scriptures of the race. It believes in the authority of the Bible, but it is the authority which truth always has over honest and candid minds.

It does not think it essential to decide when the books of the Bible were written, nor by whom; nor when they were collected and put together in the canon. The books remain the same, whoever wrote them; by giving their author another name you cannot rob them of a single note of power or of love. We are sure that the best books have remained, for they have been guarded by the love of mankind. They are not supernatural in any sense but that in which all our life is overflowed by something from above, all nature filled with a diviner beauty, and by which there is something of God in all the best things said and done by man. There is no truer word than that of Emerson: —

> " Out of the heart of Nature rolled
> The burden of the Bible old.
> The litanies of nations came,
> Like the volcano's tongue of flame,
> Up from the burning core below,
> The canticles of love and woe."

I would believe more in divine inspiration than the old doctrine allows, not less. That teaches an occasional influx from God, coming and then going away; making a few prophets in a certain land and race, but nowhere else. I believe in "the prophets who have been since the world began," in a God "who has never left himself without a witness in the world," in a light "which lightens every man who comes into the world." The old doctrine of inspiration is like a theory of water which should only tell us of the deluge, when it rained forty days and forty nights, and when the waters covered the earth. The new doctrine is like the other view of water which describes its perpetual descent in dews by night, in showers by day, — in winter snow and tropical storms, — making the whole earth glad and full of life. "For as the rain cometh down and the snow from heaven, and watereth the earth, making it bring forth seed to the sower and bread to the eater, so shall my word be that proceedeth out of my mouth, saith the Lord."

It may be said, "If we know so little about the origin of the Bible and how it came together, how can we be sure that we have the right books in it, and not the wrong ones?" There is a principle which applies in literature as well as in science, called "The survival of the fittest." The best writings are preserved by the love of mankind, — the poor ones perish. Many of the books of the Old Testament are lost. The present books appeal to them as authority, — quote the "Book of Iddo the Seer" and the "Book of Jasher," &c. But it is not probable that we have lost much in losing them. We see something of the New Testament in the process of formation. Eusebius, about 325, tells us of three classes of books, — those generally accepted, those generally rejected, those accepted by some and not by others. One of the books which has now dropped out entirely was in all the manuscripts of the New Testament till the fourth century. This was the Epistle of Barnabas.

The greatness of the Bible does not consist

in the tame monotony of one uniform revelation, the same teaching in the book of Kings as the Gospel of John; but in the very opposite, in a variety which meets every temper of the mind, every phase of life, every tone of earthly experience. There are hours of dark despair when, of all the books of the Bible, only Ecclesiastes is welcome as an adequate expression of that black mood of the soul. There are hours of bold questioning, when we call on the heaven above and the earth beneath to explain the awful enigmas of human life. And if then, in our most audacious flight of thought, we open the book of Job, we find a bolder reason than our own, one which casts aside all pious phrases and demands to know the exact truth, the whole truth, and nothing but the truth, whether God is thereby vindicated or not.

None have done more injustice to the inexhaustible volume of inspiration in the Bible than the long series of theologians who have made it their one end to put the Bible into the press of their system, and to force every part to conform to every other part. Those who find the doctrine of the Trinity in the three angels of the book of Genesis, the doctrine of total depravity in the sad wail of Jeremiah over the sins of his time; who see Anselm's doctrine of atonement typified in the Jewish scape-goat, and the Christian resurrection indicated in Job's desperate cry to God to come and vindicate him in the flesh on earth, — such theologians have done their best to squeeze the life out of the Bible, and make it as small and tame as their own shallow minds.

How much nobler is Dean Stanley, who speaks thus of the book of Esther:—

"It is expedient for us that there should be one book in the Bible which omits the name of God altogether, to prevent us from attaching to the mere name a reverence which belongs only to the reality. . . . The name of God is not there, but the work of God is." "Let those who cling to the authority of every book in the Bible be warned by this not to make a man an offender for a word, or the omission of a word. When Esther nerved herself to enter, at the risk of her life, the presence of Ahasuerus, 'I will go in unto the king, and if I perish, I perish,'— when her patriotism uttered itself in the noble cry, 'How can I endure to see the evil that shall come upon my people? how can I endure to see the destruction of my kindred?'— she then expressed, though she never named the name of God, a religious devotion as acceptable to him as that of Moses and David, who no less sincerely had the sacred name always on their lips."

Thus speaks Dean Stanley, and adds that Esther in this is the Cordelia of the Bible, the sister who refuses to use words of praise to her father, but acts her gratitude in her life.

> "Thy youngest daughter does not love thee least;
> Nor are those empty-hearted whose low sounds
> Reverberate no hollowness."

I wish the Bible to be more loved and honored than it is now, not less. I wish it more a source of faith and hope than now; to bring us nearer to God than it now does; to make Christ more interesting, and more of a true Teacher, Master, and Friend. The better we understand it, the more shall we revere it; not with a blind homage, but with an intelligent admiration. The more freely that we use our reason, separating the chaff from the wheat, the more will the genuine power and beauty of the Bible be made manifest. God, who has given the Bible, has also given us our reason with which to examine and understand it, and we are guilty before him if we bury this talent in the earth and hide our Lord's money.

If we preach a free and rational Christianity,

THE BIBLE. 49

let us do it in order to make men more religious, not less so. Teach them that God loves his children in all worlds; that if they are punished for sin, here or hereafter, it is that they may be made better; that God desires even the wicked to be as happy as they are capable of being; that suffering will be found at last to be the means of greater good; that we can begin now to love God, trust in him and serve him; that to serve him is to do good to our fellow-men; that true religion is not belief, but life; not creed, but conduct; that, since God has made us, he must have put something good in all of us, and that we ought to cultivate whatever in us is good, and so put down the evil; that God is always near us, an all-surrounding love, ready to help, inspire, and strengthen us; that true religion must be in accordance with reason, at harmony with science, art, and literature; that there can be no war between God's oldest revelation of himself in nature and what he teaches by inspired men. Teach men to see God in all things, — in the stars and the rocks, the ocean storms and the tropic calm; in the infant's smile and the mild evening of a good man's life. Thus shall we oppose best the progress of unbelief and irreligion, and of that moral death which consists in living without God in the world. Let us not be afraid of doubt, for truth can never die. Instead of thinking too much of death and hereafter, let us make a heaven here below by faithful lives, and leave our future to God in perfect submission and entire trust.

III.

GOD.

BY REV. ANDREW P. PEABODY, D.D.

"*God, even the Father.*" — JAMES iii. 9.

DID it ever occur to you how absolutely numberless must have been the patterns of all variable fabrics of human art and skill, — carpets, wall-papers, porcelain, details of finish in furniture, fashions of jewelry? Every year brings its avalanche of novelties, and yet there is no repetition; nor will there be, if the world should last as many centuries as it has lasted years, and should the civilization of its latter days demand the same sort of fabrics that we use. If you will suppose that a pattern-maker has at his command a straight line, four or five different curves, and three or four tints, the combinations that he might make of some or all of these simple elements are more numerous than man ever had the patience to calculate or to write; and with every added line or tint the figures that would express the combinations vastly exceed the preceding number, and increase so rapidly, that, with the curves and colors to be found, for instance, in what would be called a very plain carpet, they would far surpass the number of atoms in the solar system; for these are given in figures by the latest physical philosophy, while the possible patterns of which I have spoken transcend the scope of human arithmetic.

How easy, then, you might say, must be the inventor's task! No, not so, by any means; for while there are myriads of combinations that might please the eye and satisfy the taste, there are myriads of myriads that would be unsightly. Were you or I, untrained, to make the experiment, we might continue trying it for a lifetime, and for a score of lives, if they were given us, before we could hit upon a pattern that would be barely passable; for there would be millions of chances of failure to one of success. All this pattern-making is the result, not of happy chance, but of educated taste, trained eye, and practised hand.

The universe happened out of chaos, say certain (so-called) philosophers. In the swirl of eddying atoms, some impinged upon others, and became entangled with them. Thus were formed pairs, clusters, groups of atoms, which somehow blundered into life. By happy successions of chances, a portion of them attained higher modes of vitality. By still more happy chances, there grew up in some of them intelligence, reason, will, love, superstition, religion; and at length, after countless ages, by the masterly handless throw of an unloaded die came forth the supreme wisdom that can emancipate itself from religion, and rejoice in a world without a God, — this last chance, it seems to me, the strangest of all, against which I should have rated the probabilities as millions to one.

The hypothesis of a godless world carries absurdity on its very front. There are some sixty elementary substances in our earth and its atmosphere. Were you to belt the solar system with figures, you could not express the number of possible combinations of two or more of these elements. But immeasurably the greater part of these combinations would be of elements mutually incompatible, neutralizing, destructive, — many of them, against which chance could not guard, such as would make extensive havoc where there were the beginnings of organic life and development. Suppose these elements fermenting in an ungoverned chaos, the utmost that we can conceive would be, here and there, now and then, a combination that might seem to have a future, but sure to be speedily whelmed by or in some clustering of uncongenial elements that could only restore to the seething abyss what had barely emerged from it.

But what do we see? In the first place, a world stocked with organisms and inorganic compounds, each of which, to say the least, bears as clear indications of intelligent purpose as any pattern that ever came from human hands,— each of which has its seeming reason for being, in its capacity of enjoying or giving enjoyment, or in perfectly definable uses, adaptations, or relations. Nor do we find any combinations that look as if they had merely happened,— that have no reason for being, no place among the rest, no service to render or to receive. In a chance-world such could not be the case. Even were there in such a world any congruous combinations, the hap-hazard and incongruous combinations would vastly outnumber the others; for the number of them that are possible immeasurably exceeds that of the others.

But this is not all. Suppose it possible that chaos should, by the accumulation of happy chances through unnumbered æons, have been resolved into combinations that could hold together, there is an improbability which figures are inadequate to represent that any considerable number of these combinations would harmonize with one another, so as to be sub-systems of larger systems; and a still stronger improbability that these larger systems would be so correlated as to make a *cosmos*, an orderly whole, with all its parts mutually consistent, auxiliary, complementary. Yet this is what we see in our planet, — combinations in no sense dependent on one another, connected by no causative relation, yet perfectly adapted to one another, supplying to one another what each might seem to lack, — even their apparent or brief discords resolving themselves into interludes or staccatos in the grand diapason in which all created things bear part in the universal harmony. And this a chance world! with more myriads of probabilities against it than there are sands on the sea-shore, or drops of water in the ocean.

But this is not all. Astronomers have made their calculations as to the probability that various identities, proportions, and laws of the planetary orbits, distances, and motions happened by chance; they give an intensely strong numerical probability against each of these harmonies as the result of chance; and these numbers must all be multiplied together into a sum beyond conception, to represent the number of probabilities against one, that all these harmonies could have existed otherwise than by creative or co-ordinating mind, will, purpose.

Nor yet is this all. The same calculus has been extended — though, of course, in such vast spaces and distances, but imperfectly and tentatively — into the stellar universe, to the binary stars, the drift of stars in space, and various phenomena that are gradually finding record in the observatories of Europe and America, — all indicating harmonies, against untold probabilities to the contrary, were the universe self-formed and self-governed.

Now, in view of these harmonies, multiplied beyond our count to our familiar view, and extending to the utmost limits of telescopic vision, even if I had not the faintest religious feeling, or the feeblest craving for a God, my arithmetic and logic would compel me, however reluctantly, to believe in a Supreme Intelligence, all-wise, omnipotent. I should be an idiot to doubt it. Even did I say, in the perversity of a depraved heart, "There is no God," my mind would give the lie to my heart; my reason would constrain my faith. The conception of the Being mirrored alike in the rose-leaf or the insect's wing, and in the majestic courses of the heavens, is indeed, at best, faint, feeble, inadequate,— least adequate when most vivid. How, then, can we set limits to our gratitude to Him, that he has shown as much of himself as we need to know in One who bears his image, in a form human and divine, revealed while veiled in a life on the same earthly plane on which we dwell,— in One equally our Lord and our brother, offering himself at once to our familiar contemplation and love, and to our adoring reverence and admiration!

The testimony of nature to its Author being thus clear and strong, it is not surprising that a very large proportion of the foremost scientific men have been believers — many of them devout believers — in God. The late John Stuart Mill, who inherited atheism from his father, in his posthumous Essays admits that there are in the universe so many evidences of design, plan, purpose, as to render the supposition of an intelligent Creator at least probable. He thinks, too, that there are manifest tokens of benevolence in the Creator; but is inclined to ascribe to him something less than omnipotence. He had not, and has not, says Mill, entire control of the material with, by, and upon which he works. Hence the existence of Evil, which could not exist under the government of a being both almighty and perfectly benevolent. Let us attempt the problem of Evil, which has baffled the philosophy of many centuries; for, without some approximate solution of this problem, while our reasoning from design remains impregnable, and we should believe in God, we could not, with any comfortable assurance, say, with St. James in our text, "God, even the Father." If evil is beyond God's control, existing in spite of him and in contravention of his purpose, though we might be constrained to say, "Hallowed be thy name," and "Forgive us our trespasses," we could not add, "Deliver us from evil;" and a God who cannot save his creatures from, or through, or by evil cannot be their Father.

In approaching this problem I would say at the outset that, if it admits of perfect solution (as it undoubtedly does), still we must not expect any solution of ours to be entire and perfect. The limitation of our faculties and the narrow range of our observation and experience, both in space and in time, would preclude this. God alone can fully interpret God.

This premised, let us understand clearly what is implied in omnipotence. When we say that all things are possible with God, we except things that are in their very nature impossible. He cannot make two and two five. He cannot endow that which is intrinsically wrong with the characteristics of the right. He cannot make veracity, integrity, or purity sinful. Now it may be that there are certain ends, in themselves desirable, which as paramount ends are by nature and of necessity incompatible with one another; that of two valuable ends one can be pursued only by subordinating and sometimes sacrificing the other; and that in such a case omnipotence, even under the direction of infinite love, must hold the lower end in abeyance, or suffer it to fail, for the sake of the higher.

Let us, in our inquiry, consider, first, what may be necessary for the development of certain traits of character, not expressly moral, yet furnishing the surest holding-ground for consistent and persistent moral principle; namely, skill, prowess, enterprise, hardihood of nerve and spirit, — in fine, all that constitutes robust, energetic, and progressive manhood. So far as we can trace the seeds and the germinating stages of character, Eden would have been the poorest possible nursery for these traits. Its denizens could have been little better than Sybarites. The writer of Genesis gave expression to a profound philosophical truth, when he said that God cursed the ground, that is, made it unfruitful, for man's sake; for in whatever necessitates labor, man is the beneficiary. Now which is the more dignified, worthy, desirable condition, — that of physical ease and enjoyment, or that of conflict with stubborn, yet not intractable elements, with seeming evils that may by man's agency be transformed into goods, with laws and forces of nature, at first adverse, yet capable of being disarmed or utilized by science, art, resolute purpose, and energetic action? There can be but one answer.

Still farther, so far as mere happiness is concerned, the balance is decidedly in favor of the vigor, courage, and perseverance that contend with nature, and against the quiescent state of mere luxurious ease. Who has not felt this? Whence the charm of athletic sports, of arduous explorations, of perilous adventures? How is it that so many who are born and bred in affluence, and have no need of toil for their subsistence, choose modes of life fraught with labor, exposure, hardship, and danger? Whence the Kanes, the

Franklins, the Livingstones? This type of character could be developed only by what are called physical evils; and these evils can be encountered, surmounted, subdued, by intense and persevering effort, while without it they remain in full force. It is worthy of emphatic notice in this connection that nature presents no insuperable difficulties, no incurable evils, no obstacles insurmountable to human endeavor; and, also, that these adverse elements of our condition cannot be encountered once for all, but, when subdued, can be kept subject and serviceable only by a continuance of the enterprise and energy that first did battle with them. In point of fact, these evils do gradually yield to man. Many former objects of peril and dread have already been made harmless. The process is going on with many others. It is impossible to say, for instance, what immense accessions of security by land and sea will attend the growth of the still infant science of meteorology. In fine, when we take into view what has been already effected in this and many other departments, we may anticipate a condition in which man's control over nature will be almost entire and supreme, yet one in which a decline in those qualities that made him victor would unhang the trophies of his conquest, and render him again the slave and victim of the elemental forces.

Now, if physical evil is essential to the formation and growth of these noble qualities in man, we may well adopt, in an altered sense, the words which Milton puts into the mouth of the arch-fiend, and say, "Evil, be thou my good!" and may thus regard this entire aspect of nature as attesting only omnipotent wisdom and love.

As regards moral evil, a parallel course of thought is obviously just. We can conceive of a race of intelligent beings, capable of amiable and devout affections and of good deeds, yet not subject to temptation or susceptible of evil. But is not this a type of character immeasurably beneath that arduous and enterprising virtue which first subdues, spurns, surmounts evil in its own person, and then wages war with it in and for surrounding society and the human race? In the ordinary conception of heaven and its native dwellers, can the highest archangel, whose path was never crossed by the shadow of wrong, possess any thing that merits the name of goodness, as compared with the sacramental host on earth, patriots, reformers, philanthropists, prophets, apostles, martyrs,— men who, from the successful warfare within, have gone forth to stem the current of iniquity, — have yielded up substance, reputation, life, to raise the fallen, to reclaim the lost, to conquer whole provinces of humanity for truth and right, for Christ and God?

Moreover, have not these men a purer happiness, a higher joy, than a heaven of repose and monotonous worship could give? Look at St. Paul, breasting every peril, beaten, set in the stocks, imprisoned, driven from city to city, yet when in the grasp of the terrible Nero, and anticipating speedy death on the cross or in the amphitheatre, not only calm and self-possessed, but triumphant, jubilant, calling on his fellow-Christans to joy and rejoice with him.

Now, if these higher forms of character could, in the very nature of things, be produced only by conflict with moral evil, then is the sufferance of moral evil not only consistent with, but a necessary consequence of, the omnipotent love of God. Freedom of volition is, indeed, a perilous gift. It was, perhaps, impossible that it could be conferred on any race of finite beings, without their working out for themselves the disastrous moral experiments which have defaced the whole history of man thus far. It may be that more direct interposition to annul the consequences of moral evil, or to prevent its hereditary transmission, would have generated recklessness, and produced more wrong than it could remedy. Moreover, while we anticipate, with the growth of Christian civilization, a more virtuous future, it may well be that the maintenance of that better condition will still demand and nurture the same energy and potency of goodness that will have been needed to actualize it. All this is at least probable from our point of view; and it presents the only solution of the mystery of evil consistent with just inferences as to the Divine character derived from the whole structure and course of nature.

But we must not forget that there are in human experience numerous sufferings, calamities, prolonged and accumulated depressions and misfortunes, which have no offset of moral benefit, and no earthly relief or compensation; and that there are unnumbered instances of depravity in which there is no clear consciousness of the wrong or possibility of the right, yet in which retribution falls with its full weight of distress, agony, and torment. This is the night-side of humanity, on which rests not a straggling lightbeam from our lower sphere. Yet even this is suffused with rays from the Saviour's broken sepulchre. Immortality philosophy conjectures, Christ proclaims. The suffering and sin of which I have spoken are inevitably incident to the physical and moral evil from which grows all that is noblest and best in human character. It is at least conceivable — it is strange that any Christian should regard it as less than certain — that for these innocent victims of evil there will be an awakening from the death-slumber to an eternity of privilege and happiness. What will the sufferings of this earthly life then be to them? What the troubled visions of the night are, when "joy cometh in the morning." Nay more, there may be a divine alchemy by which remembrances of earthly privation and suffering may be transmuted into the elements of higher felicity, it may be even into those pure affections, desires, and aims which, whether on earth or in heaven, are the staple of all intense and enduring joy.

Without attempting to look farther between the leaves of the book which we cannot open, let me say that eternity is the adequate interpreter of the mysteries of time, not because it enables us to solve them all, but because it contains infinite possibilities of solution. At the same time, it accounts for the existence of these mysteries. If there be immortal life, then we here see only the small beginnings of things,— too minute a portion of the curve for us to determine its equation,— infinitesimals which we have not the means of integrating.

If the problem of evil admits, as we have seen that it does, of approximate solution, there remains no cloud upon the Divine benevolence; for there are in the constitution and order of nature unnumbered tokens of kind design, of beneficent purpose, — unnumbered provisions which have no possible meaning but the comfort, welfare, and happiness of man and of other orders of sentient beings; and if evil can be or seem to be the means of higher and more enduring good, we have the concurrent testimony of the material and spiritual universe to the perfect benignity of its Author. But God the Father implies even more than this, — not merely a wise and kind providence, but tenderness, sympathy, and affection for each individual human being. The father enters lovingly into all that can make the child happy, — not only into the grave concerns and emergencies of his life, but into its daily current, its festive aspects, its sport, laughter, and frolic, — takes a genial interest in all its little joys, solicitudes, and sorrows, with a readiness to enhance every pleasure, to lighten every burden, to soothe every grief. All this is implied in the Divine fatherhood. God's fatherhood, like man's, must include even the emotional recognition of the child's spiritual well-being or ill-being, — regret for his unworthiness, joy in his repentance, his resistance to temptation, his growth in goodness. Nor let us shrink from ascribing emotion to the Infinite Being. As the sea-swell is type and token of the ocean's vastness and grandeur, so is the pulse-beat of a love intense and tender far beyond our experience and thought an inexpressibly more adequate conception of the Supreme Being than the icy repose so often associated with his image.

Let us remember that it is by the inbreathing of his own spirit that there are awakened in our hearts the home-loves that are full of unutterable joy; that they gain strength by all our communion with him; that the nearer we approach him, the dearer is our affection for those whom he has given to us; and that in man nothing seems so godlike as the self-forgetting love of the greatly good, — their intense fellow-feeling with infancy in its innocent gladness, with childhood in its glee, with youth in its sinless mirth and gayety.

Nor let us forget that the father loves not only the child that deserves his love, but, if possible, even more, though regretfully and agonizingly, the wayward, disobedient, profligate child, — unwearied in his efforts to reclaim him, watching for the faintest tokens of better promise, forgiving to the uttermost when the child returns to duty and virtue. Here we have precisely the type of the Divine fatherhood as portrayed by Jesus. In his parable, it was the child who had ruined himself by vice, and had wallowed with the swine in vilest infamy, that said, " I will arise and go to my father;" and it was such a child that the father ran forth to meet, fell upon his neck with kisses, held high festival for him, and made the whole house ring with music and dancing. A father's or a mother's undying love has often won back the else hopelessly lost child; and were the Divine fatherhood, instead of being so often spoken of as the prerogative of the good alone, represented and felt as unchanged and ever genial for the worthless and abandoned sinner, — were it felt that the heart that throbs with the gladness and the grief of a sentient universe sorrows for his waywardness, and would have a new joy in his reformation, — would not this thought awaken sincere penitence in many a soul which terror cannot move, and which is perhaps hardened in guilt because it believes itself rejected, even hated, by God no less than by man?

Let, then, the title of God as a Father be held, not as a cold, heartless theological formula, but as a real, vital, home-coming truth, — one which we can best interpret from our own most intimate consciousness. God is such a father as we have known in our experience as children, as we have yearned to be to our own children, only that all that we have thus felt is to his fatherhood as the lambent tongue of flame is to the perennial fire from which it darts.

Nor let it seem unworthy of our conception of the Infinite Creator that he should be in sympathy with our small concerns, and humble needs, and paltry pleasures, — that he who dwells in the far-off heavens should yet be unspeakably near to the lowly, trusting heart. Of types of this wonderful truth the whole world is full. The little wayside flower has a life that is closely intertwined with all that is great and glorious in the universe. The vast forces of nature are its satellites and servants. The sun unfolds and paints its petals. The starry night sheds its dew upon it. The winds of heaven are its reapers and its sowers. The revolving spheres mark the cycle of its growth. Much more, then, shall not the soul of man, frail and feeble indeed, yet with the power of an immortal being, have its life-roots, its nurture, its refuge, its hope, in the vast, the grand, the infinite, yea, in Him whose being transcends space, time, and thought? What more, then, does the Divine Teacher than to give voice to nature's unwritten word, when, pointing to the lilies on the mountain-side, he says, "Shall he not much more care for you?"

Let me close with a still more emphatic reference to Jesus as the revealer of the Divine fatherhood. "He that hath seen me hath seen the Father," says our Lord. Mark, "the Father," — not a second person of a tripartite or a triune God, but the Father, whom the popular theology has so separated from Jesus in their respective relations to man, that by no possibility could either represent the other. God, as a father, could be fully manifested on earth and among men. His omnipotence and omniscience can be shared by no finite being. There can be but one Almighty, but one All-wise, in the universe. But fatherhood — perfect love and tenderness, the perpetual outgoing of kind thought, and faithful care, and offices of mercy, the yearning affection which can never count the lost as wholly lost, and which bestows only the more abundant effort and sacrifice where there is the deepest need — may have its abode in the finite spirit no less than in the one Infinite Being, may be incarnate on the earth, may dwell among men, and they may behold its ineffable beauty and glory. It has dwelt in all its fulness, its divineness, its unsurpassable perfectness, in One, and but one, in a human form. Its path on earth was thick-sown with benefits for man. It won the clinging embrace of innocent childhood. It spurned not the touch of the loathsome leper. It whelmed with unhoped forgiveness the despised and rejected of men. It sent the maniac from his lair among the tombs, to gladden his household. The dead heard its voice and lived, and the cry went forth, "God hath visited and redeemed his people." On the cross it breathed only intercessions and blessings. In death it was too strong to die, and slept in the grave only that there might grow from it the perennial spring-flowers of the resurrection.

All this Christ was and is; and in this he is the Emmanuel, the God with us, the God in man, the Father in the Son in whom is the entire fulness of his love, "God in Christ, reconciling the world unto himself." His fulness we have all seen in its faithful record; and we all must feel it, if we will only read that record with the inward eye, and give it heart-room, — yes, room and a home in our hearts for Him who so often in his mission of love had not where to lay his head.

What, then, is our Christian doctrine of God? Nature reveals him by innumerable tokens which admit of no interpretation except that of an omnipotent and all-wise Creator. Evil resolves itself into a ministry for the higher good of those in conflict with it. The Gospel proclaims more than benevolence, — a fatherhood, of which the parental love of human experience, as it is the outflow, is but the type and shadow. This fatherhood Jesus manifests in his life, in his death, in his new birth from the sepulchre to the life eternal.

Be ours not alone the tribute of our sanctuary worship, not alone our distant, awe-stricken reverence, but more, and most of all, the fervent adoration of a child's heart, the glad consecration of a child's faithful obedience and service, — an obedience which will make us almoners of all that comes to us from our Father's love, — a service in which we must needs be the followers of Him who showed himself most divine in that he went about doing good.

IV.

JESUS CHRIST.

BY REV. BROOKE HERFORD.

" *The life was the light of men.*"— St. John i. 4.

OF all the objects of religious thought there is none on which I so rejoice to speak to you as on Jesus Christ. We may differ from other churches as to what exactly was that unique personality; but we all alike look to him as, above all others, the Teacher, and, in the surpassing greatness of his help to mankind, the Saviour. In all the problem of religion, Christ is the chiefest factor. If you would work out that problem from the human side, in Christ you have humanity at its highest religious power. If we think that the problem is to be worked out from the divine side, still, of all lives and words in which we find the manifestation of the divine, Christ is the highest and clearest. Morally and religiously, he stands at the head of our race. With him began what Dr. Martineau well calls " a new edition of human nature;" and, for eighteen centuries now, the world's best life has kept referring itself back to him as its originating and sustaining influence.

There is something in all this which would make the person and the work of Christ always interesting, even as a mere historical study. But it is something far greater than an historical study. The work of Christ, as I hope to show you, is still going on; and the power of that work still lies, as it has ever done, in reverential discipleship to his person, to that word and spirit and life which constitute the Christ of the Gospels.

And now if I should describe in brief what it is that our Unitarian Churches stand for in regard to what one may call the person of Christ, I cannot put it in any better words than those which I have just used, — "the Christ of the Gospels." That which the Gospels are full of is a Life, — a life of wonderful holiness and goodness. To after ages, that life seemed so wonderful, so above any level of human living, that it became the great controversy of Christendom what it really was; and the Orthodox explanation came to be that Jesus Christ was, in reality, Almighty God. Now we cannot receive that explanation. We believe it is a mistake. But what we specially stand for is not some other explanation of our own. As a fact, our explanations are various, and some Unitarians frankly own that it is beyond their explaining. But what we want is to go back of these explanations and definitions which make up the Christ of the creeds, back to the life itself, — the Christ of the Gospels. That is where we lay the emphasis. In the Gospels, we believe that we get back the very nearest that we can to Christ as he really lived among men, and as he seemed to those who actually listened to his voice and looked up into his face. It was that life which set Christianity going in the world. In that Christ of the Gospels resides the central, undying power of Christianity.

A great question, however, meets us on the threshold. When I speak of the Christ of the Gospels as that which we should study and tie to, I am at once asked, "Is there really enough known to us about Christ's life and thought for us to tie to?" There is a wide-spread impression abroad that modern Biblical criticism has cut away the very ground of any permanent discipleship to Christ by showing that the accounts we have are not historical; that all the clear outlines of that figure which the world has bowed down to are mythical or legendary; that the whole is a half imaginary picture,—nothing to depend upon in it, nothing discernible enough to stand for.

This is an utter mistake, however. What criticism has really done is this: it has cleared away the idea that the four Gospels are inspired and infallible narratives; but it has not touched this fact: that those four Gospels, taken simply as you would take any other accounts of any other ancient life, give us such a picture of the life and spirit and word of Jesus as we have of no other life in all the ancient world! Take the extremest criticism even: suppose that not one of our four Gospels was actually written by those immediate followers of Christ whose names they bear; that it was some generations before the story of Jesus was thus written down at all. This does not affect the main facts. It does not affect the historic reality of that great figure which left such an impress on those around that even for so long, though unrecorded, it kept itself in mind so clearly and distinctly. Fortunately, we know exactly in what direction to allow for the effect of such a lapse of time and for the accretions of tradition. That was put fairly and clearly by John Stuart Mill, who looked at the whole matter simply as an outsider, certainly with no predisposition to find more in the Gospels than there really is. "The tradition of followers," he says, "suffices to insert any number of marvels, and may have inserted all the miracles. . . . But who among his disciples, or among their proselytes, was capable of inventing the sayings ascribed to Jesus, or of imagining the life and character revealed in the Gospels?" Exactly. Every exaggeration of Christ by the world must have been in the direction of the world's ideals of greatness; but then every one of those ideals of greatness, alike among Jew and Gentile, was quite different from that which the Gospels actually present to us. Judaism might have invented a grand Messianic figure; the Gentile world might have invented a warrior-patriot or a philosopher; and either Jewish or Gentile followers may have toned up the actual Christ-life in either of these directions: but neither Jewish nor Gentile enthusiasm was capable of inventing or of evolving that actual Jesus of Nazareth who went right in the teeth of both, whose life and death alike were a disappointment to the Jew and an absurdity to the Gentile. Nay, you see how the idealizing tendency did work. It gradually glorified Jesus into that grand celestial Christ, that mighty divine being which, as I shall show you by and by,

the creeds expounded. Fortunately, they were
so busy exaggerating in this direction that the
human life of Jesus was hardly meddled with at
all. That was not the line along which exaggeration was going on. So that there is good reason
to accept that human life as, in all its main features, true; and the figure of Jesus stands out
untouched by criticism, — "a unique figure," as
Mill calls him, and "in the very first rank of
the men of sublime genius of whom our race can
boast."

What a figure, what a life, that is, of which
the Gospels are full! If you only read them
casually, still it is an impression, very distinct in
its way, that they leave upon you, — the impression of a life glowing with a strange, close consciousness of God, and, in the impulse of this,
going about doing good with beautiful, tender
loving-kindness, and constantly, on the way,
letting fall teachings of deep wisdom about the
heavenly Father, and duty, and life.

When you go near, when you look carefully
into the Gospels, the features of all this keeping
take form more and more vividly. You see that
life as it came out into the public view, and went
about from place to place for a few brief years,
and then passed away. You see the surround-

ings of that life, which gave it its form: — that Jewish people, the Puritans and irreconcilables of the ancient world, looking with intensity of longing for a great political Messiah; misreading the old prophecies of the triumph of the Jewish faith into predictions of the triumph of Jewish power, and losing all the light and blessing of that old faith in the eager waiting for a mighty conquering deliverer. And among them rises up one who says: "My people, come unto me! The Lord has put his spirit upon me, hath anointed me — made me his 'Messiah,' or anointed one — to preach to you that his kingdom is at hand, and to call you to believe the good tidings, and to enter into it!" But the kingdom that he preached was not a successful Jewish revolution, but simply the drawing of all men together into brotherhood with one another, and childlike love to the great Father, and into earnest, dutiful life, and the loving even of their enemies! What a wonderful thought to come with such possessing power into the soul of one who to the people about was just Jesus, the carpenter's son, of a little Galilean village! People sometimes try to make out that Christ was simply the product of his time. No: you cannot get Christ that way! The very master-thought of his life was the very opposite to the great thought of his time, rose clear above it.

With that great, tender thought swelling within him, he went forth among his people, preaching this kingdom of God, that wanted no revolt, no bloodshed; that waited for no great national opportunity; that was right "at hand," open to every one, rich or poor, the Gentile or the Samaritan as well as to the Jew, — to every one who would believe it, and repent and enter in; yea, which was even something "within." This was God's message which was upon him, and which he wanted to tell as glad tidings to cheer the sorrowful, to save the lost, and to make all men happier and better. He cared not how he lived, nor where, so that he could gather people around him to tell them of it, or touch with its healing power some sorrowful or sin-bound heart. He loves to go much among the homes of poor men like himself; but he sits down at the Pharisee's table as readily, or goes with his new disciple, Matthew, to where a company of the shunned and hated tax-gatherers had come together to see him. People did not understand it. "This man a prophet!" said the Pharisees. "Why, he goes eating and drinking just like any common man; and eats with the unclean, too!" But Jesus went right on. At marriage festivals, at rich men's feasts, he might be seen one day; the next, wandering in lonely places, with only the crust that his disciples had saved from yesterday, and the fishing-boat or the mountain-side the only place where he could lay his head; and ever full of the tenderest sympathy, weeping with those that wept, taking up little children in his arms to bless them, pitying the leper from whom all others shrank away, and full of great thoughts, and words that have been living, glowing words ever since. Sometimes those thoughts and words came forth in great discourses to the listening multitude, like that grand charter of simple, practical, spiritual religion, the Sermon on the Mount; sometimes they flashed out upon those who tried him with their questions; sometimes they broke in upon the petty bickerings and jealousies which went on in undertones around him; and, oftenest of all, they shaped themselves into some home-spun parable, in which he held the mirror up to nature, and made men teach themselves.

" And the common people heard him gladly." They do not seem ever for a moment to have given up their old hope of a great national leader, but they hoped that Jesus would by and by throw off this disguise of a lowly teacher, and come out in the character they looked for. So they gave themselves up to the delight of his wise, kind, beautiful teachings. Very touching is it to see how they flocked about him! When the news spread that Jesus of Nazareth was in the neighborhood, the farmer left his farm, the laborers came out from the cornfields and the vineyards; the mother forgot her household cares, and, snatching up her little child, set off, with others holding by her skirts, eager to have the prophet say a word of blessing for her little one; the cripple hobbled off after the rest, blind men begged the passers-by to lead them, even the village children left their play, and hurried along. And so they came about him, and sometimes almost trod each other down in their eagerness to get within the range of his voice or the touch of his garment.

And so he went on to the end. He never swerved from his preaching of that great spiritual blessing for all men, which he wanted to substitute for the old Messianic dream of his people. Once, at least, the people tried to force him to fulfil that dream, — would have taken him by force and made him king; but he only went right away, — hid himself from them. And thus came ever a little cooling of the popular feeling; and meanwhile the priestly party, who had hated him from the beginning, grew bolder in their attacks. Still he went straight on,—straight on, though apparently his mission had failed,—straight on, though it led right to his death! And so, with a great anguish for the people he had longed to save, and could not, with a great pleading of prayer for some other way, if it might be the Father's will, but with a faith that was over all, he took up that cross in which the light of his great love for man was focussed to its most touching and imperishable brightness.

This is the Christ of the Gospels;—only the barest sketch of that great life, only the outline of those moral and spiritual features of it which no criticism can touch, and yet, still, what a life it is! I do not wonder that men have puzzled over it. I do not wonder that, when the story of it spread among heathen peoples who were familiar with the idea of incarnations and demigods, the thought grew up and gathered strength, "This must have been God!" But the whole history of the way that idea grew, and the very kind of creed-making to which it turned the Church, and the results which have followed those creeds through the ages, make me sure that it was all a mistake. I am convinced that, the more men study Christ's life as it was, the more they will come back to his simple humanity, — humanity *plus* God's spirit, indeed, but *plus* God's spirit in a way which did not make him God in any sense whatever. And, after all, in saying that men will come back to Christ's simple humanity the more they study his life, what is this but saying that his life will make upon them simply the same impression that it did actually make upon those who were spectators and companions of it? Here is the one thing which, it seems to me, there is no getting over: that Christ-life, — which, on the reading of it, our Orthodox friends think must surely have been the life of God, — to those who actually witnessed it, who saw it at its brightest, never suggested any such idea. It was all an after-thought. Even those who believe that he really was God generally admit that those who were all about him were not aware of it. To them he was simply "Jesus, the Prophet of Nazareth." Why, even such a writer as William Ewart Gladstone, one of the fairest scholars of our time, — an Orthodox Episcopalian, too, who believes from other sources that Christ was God, — frankly admits that, according to the gospel accounts, Jesus appeared to those about him simply as a man. He says: "It appears on the whole, as respects the person of our Lord, that its ordinary exhibition to ordinary hearers and spectators was that of a man engaged in the best and holiest ministries, . . . and teaching, too, the best and holiest lessons, and claiming unequivocally, and without appeal, a divine authority for what he said and did ; but, beyond this, asserting respecting himself nothing, and leaving himself to be freely judged by his words and deeds." True, he thinks it was only because of the hardness and dulness of the time that Christ did not fully reveal himself; but the important thing is the fact explained that those about Jesus did not know any thing about his being God during his life. And it is evident it was so. It does not depend upon a few texts: the whole account of how those about him regarded him and treated him shows it. You find his own family thinking him "beside himself" even for setting himself up as the Messiah ; and they go out "to lay hold on him" (St. Mark iii. 21). Evidently, the disciples had no idea of his being God, or Judas could never have betrayed him, nor Peter denied him, nor the rest forsaken him. Evidently, the Jews had not, or they never could have crucified him. No; and we have this curious corroboration of the idea of his deity having come afterward: that, a few centuries later, when it *had* come, one of the points which we constantly find theologians setting themselves to explain is, Why such a grand truth had not been made known during his life? Even Athanasius says, — and this was the common explanation, — "All the Jews were so firmly persuaded that their Messiah was to be nothing more than a man like themselves, that the apostles were obliged to use great caution in divulging the doctrine of the proper divinity of Christ." Some of those old fathers gave a more curious explanation, as, *e. g.*, Ignatius, who said that it was kept secret that the devil might not know it; and subsequent writers took up the idea, and argued that, if the devil had known it, he would have taken care not to put it into the heads of the Jews to crucify Jesus, and so would have spoiled the plan of salvation. Here, again, the explanation matters little; but the fact for which such explanations were set up is most significant. It is a fact which there seems to me no getting over. For, see: that very life, which seems, as we read of it, so far above ordinary human life that after ages thought the idea of a hidden Godhead necessary to account for it, — that life, to those who actually witnessed it, who saw its very reality and glory, never suggested any such thought.

But then I am told it was revealed afterwards. I want to know when. Because it was such a stupendous fact; so stupendous, it must have been, when it first came really upon his followers, that this Jesus with whom they had been going about was verily Almighty God; and so stupendous to the Jews, so utterly contrary to all their preconceived ideas. If it were indeed so, and if this great news of Christ having been God was to be henceforth, as it has been represented, the one thing which it is most important for Christians to believe, then all the more we must expect to find it very clearly and emphatically proclaimed.

Yet do we find it so? Why, look at the great occasions which have been recorded for us, on which the apostles gave, not some passing allusion to the gospel, but a great, marked, emphatic proclamation of it. On all those occasions they speak of their Master, but how? Take that great preaching on the day of Pentecost (Acts ii.). It is simply "Jesus of Nazareth, a *man* approved of God among you." Take that solemn setting forth of Christ by Paul at Antioch, occupying nearly a whole chapter (Acts xiii.), and how does that long address wind up? "Be it known unto you, therefore, men and brethren, that through this *man* is preached unto you the forgiveness of sins." Listen to Paul, as, at Athens, he stands before the philosophers. There was nothing in their minds to make "great caution" necessary: there was every reason why, if Christ were God, he should have so proclaimed him; nay, the very way was opened by his having found that "altar to the unknown God." But that "unknown God" whom he declared to them was simply the one Almighty; and, when he comes to speak of Christ, it is simply to say that the Almighty "hath appointed a day in which he will judge the world by that *man* whom he hath ordained." Now this is surely a remarkable fact. Can you set a few passing expressions here and there in Paul's letters and expressions, all of which are more or less doubtful, against the entire absence of any hint of Christ's deity on these great and marked occasions?

Again, there is another class of occasions on which, if Christ were God, it could hardly help appearing unmistakably. I mean, when the disciples have to speak of what are called the "offices" of Christ. Sometimes they call him "the Judge," sometimes the "Mediator," sometimes the " Ransom," sometimes as one through whom they have "forgiveness of sins." Now a strong point is usually made that Jesus could only fulfil such offices through the fact of his being divine. The explanation is, that there were two natures in him, — a human nature, by which he was " Son of man," and a divine, which made him the " Son of God." If that were so, surely we might expect to find some trace of this distinction in the New Testament; for instance, that, while the ordinary life he shared with humanity should be alluded to in connection with the name "man," or "Son of man," these more exalted offices should be ascribed to him as " Son of God." But, if you look, you find no trace of any such distinction. When Paul has to speak of him as the mighty Judge, it is simply, " He will judge the world by that *man* whom he hath ordained;" when he declares the forgiveness of sins, it is, " Through this *man* is preached unto you the forgiveness of sins." It is especially as Mediator and Ransom that our Orthodox brethren, utterly misunderstanding the sense in which Christ was so, claim that nothing less than God to mediate and save would be of any use; and yet, on the one occasion when Paul speaks of Christ as having done this, how does he speak of him? "There is one mediator between God and men, *the man* Christ Jesus, who gave himself a ransom for all" (1 Tim. ii. 5). I do not say that these expressions prove that Jesus was only man; but when you never find them making that solemn and surprising announcement that Christ was God any part of their greatest and most formal proclamations of the gospel, and when you find them speaking of the highest aspects and elements in his great work simply in connection with his humanity, and when it appears that the doctrine of his deity, said to be the most important thing of all, is never directly and clearly asserted at all, but only inferred from occasional expressions, we are surely justified in regarding it as an afterthought, the joint result of glorifying reverence and theosophic speculations.

But is this idea of Christ being *man*, then, all, it may be said? Yes: as to *nature*, I believe it is; but man, *plus* such fullest inflowing and indwelling of the divine spirit, as surely lifted him above all others. The divine life and the human life are always in contact, and in many a different degree, — from that felt nearness which in prayer we call "communion," to that overmastering uplifting and teaching which in prophet-souls we call "inspiration." I give you only my own thought now; for, as I have said, Unitarianism leaves all these as open questions to be studied, but not dogmatized upon : but to me it seems that in Christ we have this contact and communion at its highest, divinest point. It is in this that I find the secret at once of those expressions of Christ's consciousness of close, wonderful life with God, and also of the fact that he uses the very same expressions about his disciples, to teach them to seek for the same thing. Does he claim, "The words that I speak unto you, I speak not of myself"? Hear him, also, as he encourages his followers to look to God for the word to speak; "for," he says, "it is not ye that speak, but the spirit of your Father that speaketh in you." Does he speak of the spirit of the Father that dwelleth in himself? He says also to them, "He dwelleth with you, and shall be in you." Does he utter that sublimest word of all, — "I and my Father are one"? Listen to him in his prayer, and he is asking that it may be so with his disciples, too: "That they may be one, even as we are one; I in them, and thou in me, that they may be made perfect in one." Do I misunderstand all this way of speaking? Yet this is the very way in which Christ's own apostles understood it all: they found in the exaltation of their Master's life the token of what all Christian life might aspire to. Why, what a word is that which Paul uses about Christ, — "In him dwelleth all the fulness of the Godhead bodily"! We cooler-blooded modern Christians are inclined to say, That is a word about Jesus that never could be said about *man!* And so we might have thought, only that we find the very same idea applied by Paul to the Ephesians; for he writes to them the ecstatic wish, "That ye might be filled with all the fulness of God." No: we do not profess to be able to understand every word that Christ says about his close life with God. It is not likely we should. We must come far nearer to God ourselves first. But this one thing seems to stand out broad and clear on the face of the New Testament: that, in Christ's close, near life with God, just as much as in his tender, loving life with man, he was "leaving us an example." This also is part of that helpful, encouraging life which pleads with us in the Gospels, and helps man onwards and upwards to that true human life which is the very essence of salvation.

And now, if I have succeeded at all in bringing out the touching, impressive power of this

Jesus Christ, as he stands for us in the Gospels, you will more readily receive what I have now to say about his work. For it will not seem to you any small thing — any lessening of his work — to say that we regard Christ's work as entirely a moral and religious work, an influence in human hearts. We have no part whatever in that idea, so strongly insisted on by some of our Orthodox friends, of Christ having died as man's substitute; of his death on the cross having, as it were, bought mankind off from hell; of his "blood" being something to shelter behind from the wrath of God. All that seems to us a shocking perversion of the beautiful work which Christ lived and died to do. And no such work was needed. God never needed any reconciling. It was to turn man to God, not God to man, that Christ lived and died. God never needed any such "satisfaction." The only thing which can give God satisfaction is that his children leave off sinning, and try to do better. Christ's whole blessed work was simply towards this, in human hearts: to show men the infinite love of God waiting for their repentance; to help them to feel the awfulness of sin to put a new love of goodness and kindness into them; to make mankind happier and better; to set the great realities of

God's will and man's duty and destiny in the clearest light, and on an immovable foundation.

All this is what he did, and what his spirit and word are still doing with a strange, undying power. That image of Christ, simply as he was, apart from any explanation of him with the thought of his loving, merciful life, and of the things he spoke to men about, — has altogether taken a curious hold on mankind. Through long ages, during which all that the churches held up before men's gaze was the great theological Christ, glorified in heaven, still the thought of the lowly Jesus, as he went about doing good on earth, never died quite out, — still lived on, with a curious power for good. When it seemed sometimes as if the Christian Church had nothing of Christ left in it but the name, that name, quietly standing for what it ought to mean, was the strength of every reformer. That name of Christ, the fact of the Church being based on Christ, has really been the one perpetually saving and renewing power of Christianity. Wherever you find men going back, not to what Wesley preached or Calvin taught, or to what the councils decreed or the fathers wrote, nor even to what the apostles laid down, but to what Jesus Christ himself was and said, you are sure to find them coming back to broad and simple faith, and to kindly practical life. And Christ is still helping men to such life all the time. His word and spirit are a help to all kindly feeling among men, a rebuke to all anger and selfishness, to all shows and shams and pretences; and even those who most think that they reject Christianity, still speak, almost all of them, with deep veneration of the personal Jesus Christ.

There is more than this, however, in Christ. A merely beautiful character would hardly have given him that place of leadership in the world's best religious life which has been his. But, connected with that life, are great, world-wide, imperishable ideas and principles. In teaching that God is the heavenly Father of all; that all men are brothers, bound to brotherly duty and kindness; and, that the service of religion is not in this or that form of worship, but in duty and kindness and simple piety of heart, — in teaching these things, Jesus touched *a universal religion*. Never mind whether these things were entirely new things or not, — probably, indeed certainly, not entirely new, — but he brought them out with a clearness, with a simplicity, and with a power with which they had never been put before; and in so doing even though they were old stones he used, he did lay them as a "foundation," — put man's religion upon a broader, stronger, surer basis than ever before.

Let us look for a moment at that comparison which Paul uses: a "foundation;" for I think it touches very closely on the point of the paramount help which Christ is to the religious life of mankind. When we talk of laying a foundation for a building, what we want is something level, strong, that we can build upon. That foundation which you try to get is not the ultimate basis, is not the bottom of all. Underneath are all the depths of the earth-strata, of all sorts of various density and cohesion, from mere quicksand to solid rock. But you do not want to dig right down to the earth's centre every time a house is wanted to work in or live in. You lay a foundation near the surface, — a foundation of great massive stones; these are really only parts of the earth's substance; but you bring them together and set them, broadly based and levelled; and there you stand, and your building stands, if it is good building. Now, it is very much the same thing that we want in our religious life. The real ultimate basis of all religion, is, the very nature of man, — that tendency towards religion, that sense of divine and spiritual realities, which seems inwoven with the very texture of mankind's life and thinking. You find this religious nature everywhere, just as the earth is under you everywhere. As a philosophical matter, I believe that religion rests perfectly securely upon this; in the large, world-wide fact of it, always has grown up out of this, — always will. But still, for the practical building of your thoughts or mine about religion, we want the foundation making a little more definite. That religious consciousness of mankind, like the earth-strata, is of very various consistency, and not easy to build upon. We cannot for ever be referring back to the universal consciousness of man, and arguing up from first principles of thought and faith. For a deep theological inquiry, mine down to the very depths of human nature; but, for your daily living thought, you want something more practicable. And it is just this which we have in the spirit and word of Christ. In Christ, the general religious nature of man came to its broadest, highest, strongest. It does not matter how. It does not matter whether you regard that Christ-life as the finest flower of human spiritual development, or as the brightest incoming of divine inspiration; there the fact is, — a consciousness of divine realities in Christ;

a sense of God's fatherliness, nearness, love; a sense of the immortal spirit-life in man; a discernment of the principles of human duty, a clear seeing of the innermost truth about *life*, such as had never been in the world before, and never have been since. Christ believed it was his great mission from God to teach men all this; and he did teach it and live it, with a simplicity, with a clearness, and with an intense certainty and authority, which have made religion, as he so taught and lived it, a clearer, stronger, broader thing to man ever since. The great fundamental realities of religious thought and human duty have been upon a different footing since Christ came from what they ever were before. It is true that men have overlaid them with all sorts of thought-building and creed-building and form-building, which have had to come down. True; but there has ever been, in this simple Christ of the New Testament, the old foundation to refer to. And, as I said at first, all through the ages, whenever men have referred back to that, — dug down through their ecclesiastical superstructions to what Christ was and what Christ said, — they have always kept coming back to the broad, simple realities of religion.

And there is a value and help in this which

ages have not weakened. I think it is as truly a help for us to-day as it ever was in the past. There are times when we have to dig right down into the ultimate facts of human nature, to see what even Christ rests upon; but from all such deeper investigations, — from all looking abroad among the religious thoughts of the world's many peoples, and other great religions, and great teachers, — I always come back with a strengthened and confirmed sense of how, in the spirit and word of Christ, the realities of religion are laid in a broad, immovable foundation, on which I can stand and feel that I am on the very rock. Amidst all the systems with which the churches bewilder me, amidst all the mazes of the theology which the ages have built up, amidst all the perplexities of this at once speculative and questioning age, I always feel that, if I can get my foot upon some great, unmistakable thought of Christ himself, I can stand there. I am upon a sort of divine common sense, which stands from age to age, solid and plain and strong.

And I want you, further, to notice that this help which we have from Christ, in the subject of religion, is only the counterpart of the help which we frankly acknowledge and rest upon in various other parts of life. In every branch of study, of thought, of action, there is such a thing as going right down to abstract first principles; but we do not practically do it. We do it now and then for a philosophical investigation perhaps, but not for the practical purposes of life. In every branch of study or action, what we practically do, is, to accept some strong, broad, clear foundation which we find already laid long ago, by some great thinker of the past; and we build on that. In every branch there has been thus some strong, massive foundation laid. What is the practical foundation on which political economy has been built? Adam Smith's great work, "The Wealth of Nations." Who laid the foundation of all this infinitely varied modern science, that with microscope and note-book goes up and down the earth, observing facts, and from them generalizing laws? Every one acquainted with the history of thought at once answers, "Lord Bacon." See, I can give you an instance closer still. What is the "foundation that has been laid" in geometry? That little work, over which I suppose most of us puzzled when at school, — puzzled until the beauty of its great principles dawned on us like a revelation, — that little work, "Euclid." What is it? That is the book which from before the time of Christ has been the practical foundation of geometrical study. It is simply the work of a man named Euclid, who, some three hundred years before Christ, was one of the professors in the great schools of Alexandria. So close is the parallel: you could imagine some admiring student of that old mathematician writing, in Paul's very phrase, " Other foundation of mathematics can no man lay than that is laid, which is this work of Euclid." It would have seemed very presumptuous, no doubt; but see, it has turned out to be the fact! That work has stood as the one sure foundation of geometrical study for nearly three centuries longer than Christianity; and it is standing yet! It is men's practical starting-point, in that matter. When they can set their feet on a " Q. E. D." of Euclid, they look no further: they feel they are about on the rock. And all students feel that the world owes a marvellous debt of gratitude to that old Egyptian teacher, who, though it was no new truth he was laying down, but simply some of the everlasting relations of things, yet so unveiled those everlasting relations, so put them in a simple way evident to all, that ever since they have been one of the steady lights of man.

When you think of that, it may not seem quite so absurd as some would regard it, that we should still have to look for the great broad foundation of our religious thinking, almost, though not quite, as far back. It is a far higher subject, that of this vague, mysterious life of ours and its invisible qualities and relations, than that of the mere relations of squares and circles; and its wisdom depends on a different set of perceptions. But yet Christ has set the great, broad realities of faith and duty in that same clear light, on that same solid foundation, as the Old World mathematician set the relations of lines and squares and circles. The great truths of the Sermon on the Mount are as universally accepted as Euclid's axioms! The meaning of the parable of the Good Samaritan is as certain as that of the forty-seventh proposition — and a great deal plainer!

Nor am I speaking of this as a mere theoretical help. It is a most practical one. It is just the very help we all of us want, in the weakness and uncertainty of our own personal discerning. I suppose there are hours when God and duty and immortality seem clear and real to our hearts. We feel them for ourselves. We do not need any one, not even Christ, to show them to us. Perhaps, if we could fix our hearts into that frame of settled faith, we should not need any helper, least of all need to look back so far for one. But we cannot so fix our hearts. There come other times when all seems dim and uncertain to us. Cold shades of doubt are over us; sometimes the mist of sin and sinful feeling hides every thing from us. Which is the truth, which corresponds to the reality?—the happy faith of the brighter hours, or this closed in blindness and vacuity of our darker? Those are the experiences in which I, for one, feel it an unspeakable help to be able to fall back upon that great word of life which we have in Jesus Christ. When all is dark about my own life, there always seems light there. I do not say that we have there all that man's ever onward thought needs. I do not pretend to find there ready-made answers to all the questionings of life. Christ is not the whole building, but he *is* the foundation. Amid the speculations of the schools, amid the tottering structures of the creeds, amid all the dimness and wavering of our personal faith, here is solid ground. Here are the great fundamentals of duty and faith, the thought of God, the hope of everlasting life, put into words of matchless simplicity and force, and wrought into the changeless likeness of earth's most perfect life. That "life," *is* "the light of men." And still along the centuries comes borne to us his pleading call, — not to adore him, but to follow him: "Come unto me, all ye that labor and are heavy laden, and I will give you rest." And still, in our true hours, when we see clearest through the maze of care or doubt, our hearts cry back to him: "Lord, to whom else should we go? Thou hast the words of eternal life."

V.

MAN.

BY REV. GEORGE W. BRIGGS, D.D.

"And when he came to himself, he said, I will arise and go to my father." — LUKE xv. 17, 18.

COMING to our subject not as the partisans of a sect, but as seekers after truth, what affirmations can we make respecting human nature? In the study of the nature of man, we must first scrutinize its manifestations in human character. All science deduces its theories from materials gained by observation. The student listens to the teachings of Nature herself in the appearances and facts of the universe, and thus discovers the laws which they illustrate and reveal. Follow the same method here. Observe the moral developments of humanity just as they are. Open the Book of Life; unloose its seals. At once, we are struck, appalled, by the terrible contrasts recorded upon its pages. It is not all glory, it is not all shame, but a confused, perplexing mingling of both. Here are generosity and meanness, truth and falsehood, honesty and fraud, heroism and cowardice, set over against each other in all life and history. Look at individual men, and you see generous and selfish feelings displacing each other upon their faces, and threads of good and evil mingled in the warp and woof of character. Look into the world, and you find homes that are gardens of joy, lighted up by a love that rejoices to live, and even to die for the child; and homes that are hells, in which fathers, mothers, living only for their own brutal appetite and passion, leave the child in nakedness and starvation. Go into crowded cities, and shrines of prayer are side by side with the haunts of the tempter, and cross-bearing towers overshadow dens of infamy. The incorruptible men and the villains, seducers plotting devilish wiles to lure innocence into ruin, and redeemers devising means to save, walk the same streets. Every creation of fiction has its hero and its villain, presenting both aspects of humanity, finding the original of both pictures in actual life. Into what opposite realms of life humanity sinks or soars! With what dramatic power these contrasts are forced upon us in our own experience! I have heard of two men born and nurtured in the same town in my native State, who breathed the same air and looked upon the same beauty of field and shore and sea. One plunged into crime, and in early manhood was doomed as a pirate to the scaffold. The other wooed truth with loving heart, and poured out his inspiration in an eloquence that entranced listening souls on both sides of the ocean; and, being dead, is living and speaking still. It is like the contrast between Judas and John. How often the grandest deeds are written on the same page with the basest! When lately a noble steamship suddenly sank, and some in the cowardice of selfish fear deserted or thrust back the perishing, the hero-captain, forgetting self in saving others, stood at his post, and went down with his ship into the devouring sea. Sometimes the grandest qualities suddenly blaze out in lives that have seemed basest. A pilot, reckless, licentious on the shore, holds the helm of the burning vessel, like a martyr at the stake, till his arms shrivel, and he perishes in his endeavor to guide her to the river's bank. Purified as by fire, such a soul ascended in a chariot of flame. Great deeds not only appear in contrast with what is basest, but are inspired by it. In the darkest ages of corruption there have been reformers, prophets, heroes. We read of tyrants and oppressors, but they called out patriots, emancipators. We turn to times of persecution, and lo! the noble army of martyrs. The shame and glory of humanity meet our eyes everywhere; and though in the book of human life deeds are recorded over which the very heavens might weep, noble, heroic, divine things are also written there at which heaven itself must rejoice.

What theory can be deduced from such opposite manifestations? One thing, at least, is proved. There are noble traits in humanity as well as base. There is good in man as well as evil. It has been too common to emphasize his frailty and baseness in theories of his nature, and overlook or disparage his grander qualities. Every such theory is indefensible, untrue to fact and life. Cowards, traitors, are not to be numbered, and heroes forgotten. What kindness, what sincerity, what honor, what courage, are seen lighting up the face, giving beauty to life! What quick sympathies there are, what melting compassions! Bring the tortured sufferer before its eyes, and humanity is at his mercy, compelled by the necessity of its nature to give relief. What love exists, forgetting self in plans, toils, life-long sacrifice! Is it said these are merely instinctive, natural graces? Intermittent they certainly are, needing to be cherished, enlarged, in order to become graces in the grandest sense, unfailing attributes and inspirations. But what must be the soil to which such flowers are native? The good belongs to humanity, certainly. Remember the men who hold fast their integrity and their honor in all possible revolutions of fortune, brave to meet financial ruin rather than swerve a hair's breadth from right. Remember the virtue in man and woman, that amid temptation repeats the victory of the wilderness. Remember the patience, fortitude, trust, ennobling lowly places. Remember the great names that illuminate history, men of ancient days and heathen faiths, who feared God according to their light, and wrought righteousness; the sages, moralists, founders of religions, whose precepts of duty shame Christendom. Remember the men of later time, the true saints, devotees not of forms but of righteousness, both within and without the pale of Christian communions; souls all instinct with thoughts of charity, or fired by a quenchless love of liberty; heroes battling, dying for human rights, philanthropists toiling, suffering to right human wrongs. Who were these but men unfolding qualities whose germs are sown broadcast in the soil of human nature? If you write on the roll of humanity the names of Nero, Caligula, Judas, write also the names of the Antonines, Howard, John.

We advance another step. If the actual manifestations of human nature are so diverse, so contradictory, comprehending both divine and infernal qualities, which is its truer development? For which was it made? The answer comes from humanity itself. And, first, which does it accept as its representative? Which does it honor? The instinctive reverence of humanity turns towards its preordained king as the needle to the pole. Is it said that men have venerated base ideals, worshipped false gods? The conceptions of duty vary, and the virtues of one age may be the sins of a later day. Still in each it was virtue, or what was then deemed so, that commanded reverence. In all times, rude or enlightened, in the inspiring words of Paul, all nations of men were made of one blood to seek and feel after God, if haply they might find him. That instinct is as innate in human nature as the instinct of the child to feel after the mother's breast. Humanity gives one unvarying verdict. It pronounces the heartless man inhuman. It scorns the traitor, and venerates the patriot. It execrates the villain, and canonizes the saint.

The very word *inhumanity* is the testimony of mankind recorded in language itself; a testimony more enduring than the statues of stone that symbolize its reverence for the great and good. The answer is always coming in the soul itself, and in human history. Which do we accept as the true types of human nature, — criminals whom society imprisons, the hollow-hearted, grasping, often more corrupt than the criminal himself, or the frank, generous, self-forgetting, whose lives touch us to admiration or tears, and take the soul captive for ever? Which does history honor, — the politician trimming his sails to catch the shifting breezes of popular feeling, the demagogue catering to discontent, ignorance, vice, sitting in the temple of legislation to shape law itself for his own ends instead of the public weal, or the man who has " an oath registered in heaven " of loyalty to right, liberty, country? These self-seekers know themselves to be base. Could they be confronted by men clothed with patriotism and righteousness, as the money-changers in the temple were confronted by Jesus, it would need no scourge to drive them from the seats which they profane: self-judged, lashed by the whips of conscience, they would go to their own place. Still, though they do not sentence themselves, fearful and inevitable are the judgments of history. The verdict of the moment is often mistaken; but the verdict of ages is just, awarding to the servants of right and man their meed of honor, dooming the self-seekers to eternal scorn.

But the answer of humanity itself to the question, which is its true development, is given in its own essential qualities. There are great moral characteristics inherent in its nature, inseparable from it, that give the same reply. Whence comes this sublime idea of justice, never silenced, for ever demanding more perfect recognition in society, law, government, overthrowing tyranny, uprooting slavery; sometimes prompting ignorant men, maddened by real or fancied wrongs, to act in a blind fury, but always, in its veriest madness, dreaming that it is laboring for juster institutions, a nobler victory of the right? Whence comes the grand thought of serving truth and justice for their own sake, without regard to reward, because they are in themselves sacred? Here is a thought shaming many a representation of religion itself, pictured in the old legend of the monk who wished to destroy heaven and put out the fires of hell, in order that men might learn to live righteously, neither bribed by hope nor impelled by fear. And whence, too, are these conceptions of God himself, of his infinity, truth, justice, love? Is it said that they come to us from without? Quickened they are by outward revelations, unfolded into strength and beauty, as the seed into plant and flower by the agency of nature. But no such ideas could be gained unless their germs were planted within us. The pure in heart see God. What power must be inborn to enable it to attain such a vision of the infinite? Man has a universe of influences like angels to attend him, and call the universe of truth in himself into life. Once more, what is the conscience itself, which, though blinded, mistaken, brings the divine idea of duty, and is a power in ourselves that makes for righteousness; which, though seared, transiently silenced, never dies; which blanches the cheek with fear, and causes the knees to smite together, and writes letters of doom on palace walls; which sees stains upon the murderous hand that would turn the ocean red, and wrings out the cry, "Which way I fly is hell: myself am hell"? Here are not merely proofs of grand moral elements in human nature, but their actual manifestations, not to be set aside in our theories, but recognized as attributes of man's truer self, — the self that makes him a man, for ever answering the question respecting his normal development.

And the same answer comes even in man's degradation. Does any one say such views overlook his actual sinfulness? If his noble traits prove inherent nobility, do not base ones equally prove inherent baseness? We shut our eyes to no degradation, no beastliness of appetite and passion; to no tendencies to secret sins of pride, envy, hatred; to no possibilities of crime. Rather do we set them in order before us in their atrocity, and look down into the hells, to learn what humanity answers for itself even there. If, as one theory asserts, man has been gradually developed from a lower type of being, the long centuries have not yet removed all traces of his ancestry. The mark of the beast is not erased. The catalogue of sins is of interminable length, and deeds of unmitigated horror are recorded there. New ingenuities of crime are reported with every morning's sun. We hear of outrages that seem to transcend the possibilities of human depravity, the work of fiends. It is not only terrible deeds that appall us. Tendencies to evil seem inwrought in many a life, ready to reveal themselves amid temptation, as lurking tendencies to disease develop into deadly activity in the noxious air.

There are transmitted qualities of evil also, inherited appetites, that a spark may kindle into consuming fire. Thank God, the good men do is not interred with their bones, though under the great law of heredity the evil also lives to curse those who come after them. Born in iniquity, with the stamp of wicked or brutal parentage on their organization itself, cradled in shame and crime, there are those whose depravity seems foreordained, inevitable, hopeless. Yes, and even in lives cursed by no such hereditary tendencies, stained by no flagrant vices, the workings of sinful feeling often show the trail of the serpent. A distinguished preacher speaks of the naturalness of the question of the disciples, " Lord, is it I?" when Jesus said, "One of you shall betray me." The suggestion of such a crime led each to conceive and tremble at possibilities of unknown evil in himself. No man rightly estimates himself if, when he unrolls the life even of grosser sinners, he does not feel that in their circumstances he might have been like them. How many are sheltered from temptations that might have ruined them! " Is it I?" Is it a true brother, his nature like mine, only differing in the circumstances, temptations of his life, who did, or is doing, these revolting, damning deeds? In him do

I see myself in a lot like his? Take into view all the facts and possibilities of human sinfulness, but still repeat the great thought of Paul, It is not I, the real self, but the sin that has for a time overmastered me. It is not the real self, but the demon that possesses it. Believe with Paul in an inward man that delights in truth and righteousness. The wrong-doer repudiates his own life as false to himself, as to God. What is remorse but the solemn judgment of the true upon the false self? What more touching revelation of man's nature than the longings, prayers, tears of the transgressor himself, willing to bear any punishment if the child can be saved from his own fall? Tortured by the thought of betraying innocent blood, self-judged, self-condemned, Judas hangs himself. Coming to himself, the prodigal goes back to his father. Tormented by the memory of his base life, the rich man in hell remembers his brothers in his father's house, and pleads that a messenger be sent to warn them. Out of the deeps of depravity and hell, human nature gives the same answer. Not the debased, but the noble, the heroic men, are its true representatives. Even great men and great ages are not miracles in history, but occasional outshinings of powers always existing in human souls. In grand lives and heroic men, Providence gives an illustration of what it is to be a *man*. Perhaps we may say, even in respect to intellectual greatness, that the difference between ages of darkness and of light is not so much in gifts of genius as in the slumber or activity of human thought. In periods of brilliant mental achievement, in men whose names are classic, seeds of genius ripened such as often lie dormant and never unfold into beauty.

> "Perhaps in this neglected spot is laid
>   Some heart once pregnant with celestial fire;
> Hands, that the rod of empire might have swayed,
>   Or waked to ecstasy the living lyre."

But if the position is questioned in this particular, it is beyond denial in respect to spiritual greatness. Who were the brave and true in peril and persecution? Were they not men? What heroism burned in workshop and farm, in hearts and homes, in man and woman, when called to defend a flag more priceless than life, — a flag worthy to bear the stars? Who were they that seem to stand near the cross itself? Not the select minds of history. Unlearned fishermen became apostles, martyrs. Gentle maidens, shrinking from the gaze of men, braved the lions and yet more savage men. Many a mother stood by the cross of her son, as " Mary stood the cross beside." Were these spirits sent down from heaven, or are they typical of our common nature, of what you and I might be? Faith in a sublime truth, loyalty to a great purpose, will make the faces of men shine like the sun, and their raiment white as the light. These true souls are the normal examples of our humanity; and we are but shapes and forms, and not men, if we do not aspire for a life like theirs.

Accept the affirmations which human nature warrants in its instinctive reverence for right and virtue, in its inherent characteristics, in the verdict which it for ever gives against its own degradation. Are they confirmed by Scripture? Not only are they confirmed, but emphasized, enforced. First, the Bible speaks of human character rather than of human nature. It draws vivid pictures of human wickedness. Studying its histories, reading the rebukes of prophets, we picture to ourselves periods of degeneracy, when, in the intense language characteristic of Scripture, men had all gone out of the way, "none doing good, — no, not one." Yet all the while there were men who hurled out these indignant rebukes, witnesses for truth and right; and every such indictment against man was drawn by man himself. If Paul, speaking of the actual condition of the Gentile world, out of which converts had been brought, says, "We were by nature children of wrath, even as others," he also says, "Gentiles who have not the law do by *nature* the things contained in the law, and show the work of the law written in their hearts." What a grand assertion of the truth that there is a law written upon the soul itself which ordains righteousness! Peter, consciously or unconsciously, recognized that truth in the brave words, brave even now, "In every nation he that feareth God, and worketh righteousness, is accepted with him." Jesus asserted it when he said, "They shall come from the east and the west, the north and the south, and sit down in the kingdom of God." The Bible is not the narrow book that men have made it. It recognizes but one thing, — righteousness; and whether men do by *nature* what righteousness demands, whenever and however they attain to it, they belong to the one fold of the one shepherd. And now we turn directly to the teaching of the true leader, Jesus. It has been justly said that the gospel is far removed from a low view of human nature. It is significant that not one of the passages chiefly cited to prove its depravity came from the lips of Jesus. On the contrary, every thing in his teaching and life implies or asserts its worth and greatness. First, what an estimate of it is involved in his own mission and work. He toils, pleads, dies, for a nature worthy of all that labor and sacrifice. No price is too costly, no cross too heavy, if humanity can be brought back to itself. A divine idea of its worth and sacredness is the only solution of such a ministry. And, next, what a sublime view of it his teachings imply and confirm! Hear his words: "It is not the will of your Father in heaven that one of these little ones should perish;" and, again, "Joy shall be in heaven over one sinner that repenteth more than over ninety and nine that need no repentance." What a picture it suggests to the imagination of the countless throng of the loving and pure watching the life of one straying soul in infinite longings; even the heavens grieved at its wandering, rejoicing at its return! But the proof of Christ's estimate of human nature is revealed even more clearly, if possible, in the way in which he appealed to it. The royal distinction of his teaching is that it manifested a trust in humanity which, even now, we scarcely begin to comprehend. To whom did he speak in the sublime words of the Sermon on the Mount, in precepts and parables, in synagogues and villages, by the lake and in desert places? To Pharisees, Scribes, the learned of Palestine, indeed; but also to lowly fishermen, the despised, the outcasts. "And the *common* people heard him gladly." Humble, simple natures drank in his words as the earth drinks in the dew. Jesus gives no theories of God or man. He embodies his conception of God in the word *father*. He reveals his idea of man by the method of his teaching. When he who "knew what was in man" presents the sublimest truths to the humblest minds, his view of humanity becomes as clear as the noon-day. What statement so conclusive as such a trust? Better than the most emphatic declaration that we are the children of God is it to be welcomed as sons, to have the treasures of truth opened to us as our inheritance, and be recognized as heirs. Remembering the way in which Jesus spoke to men, often drawing the highest truth out of their own minds, presenting it always as a teaching which, though before unknown, their nature was made to receive, we are led to the thought that even his sublime words are but the full revelation of the light lighting every man that cometh into the world, what each must see for himself as he gains the same spiritual life.

And if the words of Jesus are the words which the soul was made to receive, — its own words, in its true estate, — we can understand the name applied to him, "Son of man." Son of man! Humanity has had grand illustrations of its truer self in heroes, prophets, martyrs, saints; but Jesus incarnates its ideal purity and beauty. When you ask what humanity is, do not look at it when dwarfed by ignorance or debased by sin. I borrow Robertson's illustration. If you wish really to know a tree, you do not take its stunted specimens in a barren soil or in arctic cold: you look at it in a genial climate, putting forth its majesty as the monarch of the forest. So, when studying humanity, in order to learn its nature, you look upon him who was the Son of man.

And yet one more step remains to complete the Christian view of human nature. To be a Son of man is to be a Son of God. There is no merely speculative, but the most profoundly spiritual, significance in these two appellations applied to the same person. Here is a view which I know not how to express. But all culminates in this: that to be really a man is to be a son of God, — not his creature, but his child; that our higher nature is like his nature, that our love is a spark from his love, our sense of right and justice an inspiration from him; in one word, bewildering as it is, that we are "partakers of the divine nature," made to receive the life of God, and, in every point in which the finite can resemble the infinite, reflect his glory. It is this *mortal* that must put on life and immortality. "Now are we the sons of God, and it doth not yet appear what we shall be, but we shall be like him; for we shall see him as he is."

Do you ask what are our affirmations respecting man? We affirm what human nature affirms in its nobler or baser workings, what Christianity affirms in the words Son of man and Son of God. Never disparage a nature once incarnated in Him who is the model and the despair of the centuries. Reverence it in the weakest, and minister to it as to the Lord himself. Never overlook its actual and possible degradation, brutality, selfishness, and passion, when it so often needs regeneration to reawaken it to life. Yet still believe in it even in the basest, in the true self, imperishable in the prodigal's abandonment, sure to revive as he is perishing with hunger in some period of his history, and realize the picture in the great parable of Jesus. Honor it in yourself till you see how unpardonable it is to throw away the great possibilities of manhood and fall into meanness, deceit, self-seeking, the damning loathsomeness of appetite and lust, — unpardonable as the sin against the Holy Ghost. Yes, remember and fear the possibilities of evil, and compass yourself about with all helps, human and divine, till you can look up and say, Father, in the sweet assurance that you are his child.

VI.

THE CHURCH: THE SOCIETY WHICH JESUS GATHERED.

BY REV. RUFUS ELLIS, D.D.

" Where two or three are gathered together in my name, there am I in the midst of them." —MATT. xviii. 20.

THE subject of my sermon is the society which the Master of Christians gathered. Jesus did not write. He trusted in the supreme Spirit, and in that spoken word which his own life illustrated and enforced. He committed his work to a living, life-giving, and immortal congregation of faithful men and women, who by him did believe in God which raised him from the dead and gave him glory. Their minds and hearts were the good ground in which the Son of man sowed the good seed that should spring up and bear fruit world without end. This, under God, was the Lord's dependence, — the hiding-place of his power; at once the ever-proceeding Spirit and the ever-renewed and ever-growing body of the everlasting religion.

Evermore invisibly, as for a little while visibly, he should be the head of this society, quickening, guiding, comforting. So he finished, and again began the work which was given to him to do, and provided for those spiritual and moral triumphs which came and are to come. This was the little flock to which it was the Father's good pleasure to give the kingdom without end, the Church of the living God, the Pillar and Ground of the Truth from the time when, as we read in the Book of Acts, the names of the disciples were about one hundred and twenty, to the present hour and its hundreds of millions. It might well have seemed to human eyes a slender dependence. In that little company, not many were mighty, not many were wise. Not one of them could bear to hear what their Master had to tell them. Fulfilment, not destruction, was his method; and they might be slow to discern between what was to pass away and what was to remain and to be the germ of the new creation. But he had come to those who had received him, and he gave them power to become children of God; and his spirit in their minds and hearts was the inexhaustible source of moral and mental growth. We know their works, and our incalculable debt to them: how they gath-

ered and sifted and put into such order as was
still possible the priceless Christian traditions
and writings, the little tracts that were to replace the books of philosophy, and to be a new
Bible for the world; how the life in them took
body and form for coming ages, and beautiful
Christian usages became sacraments, and orders
for a day, which, as they thought, was far-spent,
abiding ordinances; how, whilst they waited and
longed for their world to come to an end, they
so wrought and suffered and grew in all graces,
that their world, which seemed just ready to
perish, could not come to an end, but entered
upon a new age, — and so swiftly and earnestly
that, when the earliest Christian writings (the
Epistles of Paul) begin to appear, the Church
has already made great strides towards the possession of its promised inheritance, and a vast
multitude gathered into the purest and sweetest
light which can shine for the children of men
have another king, — one Jesus. In the providence of God, this has proved to be the Assembly of assemblies, the Church of churches.
He who setteth the solitary in families, and
gathers the church in the house, which is the
Home, and the church in the wilderness, which is
the State, binds his children together at last, one

body in Christ, which is the church of the living God. In its rudiments, this society has existed from the earliest times and amongst the rudest people. From the very dawn of civilization, men and women have gathered before God, and, as in the presence of the Unseen, drawn in some way past our finding out to the mysterious Power whose nature and name are so hidden from them, but whose works everywhere meet their eyes and stir their thoughts, and of whose voice in their hearts they begin to catch faint, far-off whispers. All this is now fulfilled. "The field," said Jesus, "is the world." He gathers and inspires not a school of philosophy, nor a little knot of admiring, loyal followers, to quote and comment upon his words ever after. He and his shall be the salt of the earth; he and his, the light of the world in all its ages,— a light shining brighter and brighter unto the perfect day. It is the necessity of his eternal Sonship, the law of his spiritual and moral life. He passed from the Cross to the Throne of Glory, to be judge of the nations as inevitably as the sun climbs into the noontide sky. He is a king, and can be no other. He stands between us and God, not to separate us from him, but to bring us to him, with his open-eyed consciousness of the Father, his perfect sonship, his absolute trust in holy love, his singleness of heart and life, his love unto death for the Father's children, and his life and light, are the life and light of men, — our life and light, here and now.

And, as I say, I wish to speak to you of the society which Jesus gathers; of the spirit which is to be its inmost and essential life; of the simplicity of its form and methods; and of the pressing human needs which this life and this simplicity are abundantly able to meet.

1. And, first, of its inmost and essential life. What this must be, we gather from the Master's own lips. We read that once there went great multitudes with him, and he turned and said unto them, " If any man come to me, and hate not his father and mother and wife and children and brethren and sisters, yea, and his own life also, he cannot be my disciple." So he distinguishes those who go with him from the true discipleship, for which alone, in a movement of world-wide proportions, he holds himself accountable. The disciple, like his Master, must have no life that he calls his own. He may not separate himself from God, as if the Father's business did not always take precedence of every other work. One supreme affection, one absolute trust, one

absorbing, consuming desire, must give the law to the true follower. Less than this might suffice for other undertakings, but would be found absurdly and even ignominiously inadequate for an enterprise which proposed no less than the conquest of a world; as if one should leave an unfinished tower as a monument of his thriftlessness and folly, or go out with ten thousand to be defeated by one coming against him with twenty thousand. For the great body which we commonly call the Church, better or worse, Jesus is not responsible. It is ours, not his. He did not found it: he does not and never did depend upon it. To an enormous, amazing, and deplorable extent, it is entirely aside from and contrary to his aims and methods; and, though it contains the discipleship, is not the discipleship. It is only another, and often a worse, world,— one of the institutions to be reformed, and not seldom one of the worst accomplices in the wrong-doing of men and nations. Regarded. as an establishment, it may be a serious question whether it has not done more harm than good. Understand me: I am not arraigning the Church; I am not blind to her providential mission; I can easily admit that Christendom is at least good missionary ground, by reason of the light which rays out from many a faithful Christian congregation into the darkness around: but the multitude which go with Jesus must not be confounded with the discipleship. Take the better sort, even of this multitude, — the serious, the devout, the conscientious, the kindly, the generous, — the people who, on the whole, are favorably distinguished from those in the nations who profess the non-Christian religions, and it is very easy and very necessary to distinguish them from disciples, as Jesus defined and depicted them. Doubtless, the Lord, beholding them, loves them; but as he loved the young man who had not the heart to follow him, and was sorry for his short-coming, but not sorry enough to enter upon a nobler life. Where would Christianity have been, if its first company of disciples had been only average Christians? They had no silver and gold, that they should make collections and subscribe to missions, and send others to preach in their stead. Such a religion would never have got even to Antioch to be baptized as Christianity. Excellent and useful person as your every-day Christian is, engaged in his daily and engrossing work, occupied with his unceasing round of summer and winter amusements, fulfilling, as he says, his duties to society, — yes, even at his devotions, with his cushion to sit upon, his hassock to kneel upon, his prayer-book with the gilded cross on the outside of it to read from, his fastidiousness as to the weather, the distance, the companionship, and all the other conditions of church-going, there would be something incongruous to the verge of absurdity in applying to him the language in which this homeless man at once invites and repels discipleship. Let the Church plead her own cause. She is in possession, and should not find it difficult to keep possession; but this can be in the end only as she becomes more and more a discipleship. The true followers can only bless mankind. If any venture to talk about the fanaticism, the neglect of household and social duties and charities, the overshadowing of this world, which also is one of God's worlds, which must proceed from such exceeding, and, as they will say, extreme devotion to Christ,—I answer, unhesitatingly, that all this has come, not from a pure Christianity, but from the want of it; not from loving God supremely, but from living a life centred upon self; not of forsaking all and following Jesus, but of man's untrustful and persistent keeping back,—and not least in the church, what belongs to God, his trying to save his own little life of passion, prejudice, opinion,

THE SOCIETY WHICH JESUS GATHERED. 135

station, culture, wealth, instead of taking his share in God's life of truth and charity. Fanaticism in the name of religion, what we call the abuse of Christianity, is the characteristic, not of the discipleship, but of those who go with Jesus; not of disciples, but of ecclesiastics.

2. And now let me say, further, that, as the discipleship is to be distinguished from the vast multitude who profess and call themselves, or are called, Christians, so the simple and only essential forms and methods of discipleship may be most profitably distinguished from our great ecclesiasticisms. From the beginning of the Christian world, Jesus gathers his church not only into one great congregation of every name and nation, but into many and unnumbered congregations; and each one of these, be it larger or smaller, is a true Church of Christ, if it be indeed of his gathering and inspiring, "met in his name," it may be "two or three," it may be two or three hundreds, it may be two or three thousands. It is enough that they are mastered by him, possessed by his thought, docile to his methods, resolved to obey him and to win the world to his obedience. If any asks, "Who gathered this church?" it is enough to say, "He who in all these lands and these ages, which are called

Christian, has been gathering churches,—the one who is our Master." "The visible Church of Christ," says the nineteenth of the Thirty-nine Articles, "is a congregation of faithful men, in the which the pure word of God is preached, and the Sacraments be duly ministered according to Christ's ordinance, in all those things that of necessity are requisite to the same." According to this definition, the local congregation is as truly the Church of Christ as the vast company of Christians the world over. Of course, congregations may well confer together and act together, and be a body of Christ, just as individual Christians. And yet in the last resort, whatever authority in controversies of faith, or power to decree rites and ceremonies, belongs to universal Christendom, inheres in the local congregation, because the local congregation is as truly and essentially the Church of Christ as the whole of Christendom. Christianity is not a philosophy or a scholasticism. It is the light of life,—plain truth for plain people; and it commends itself to every hungry heart, and to every man's conscience in the sight of God.

And we want to understand that, according to the simple rule of Jesus, this church may be yours and mine. We want to understand what a church as simply constituted as this may and ought to propose and do, without waiting for the indorsement of any hierarchy. However imperfectly organized and certified such a church may seem to the ecclesiastic, the Spirit of the Lord will so empower and command the least of his little flocks, that the world shall recognize in them churches of Christian disciples; and nothing is so much needed in Christendom to-day as precisely these Christian congregations, simple in their forms, but of a divine life.

3. And yet the Christian congregation as a society, inspired, authorized, and organized for Christian work, one body and one mind and one spirit, each member of royal and priestly estate, heir of the promise which was made, not only to the individual disciple, but to Christians in council, living a corporate life, — in a word, the congregation which Jesus gathers, — is not the power it ought to be to-day in Christendom. This church is not fulfilled in an assembly for listening to preaching, or for the observance of Christian ordinances, in a mere audience or company of worshippers scattered, it may be, each to his own, with or without greetings, when service and sermon are ended; nor yet in the annual meeting of pew-hirers or pew-proprietors; still

less in the occasional coming together of some vestry, standing committee, or board of trustees. Even the conference meeting, which still lingers, is not the congregation; for it is almost exclusively pietistic, — if one may use the word in no invidious sense, — and brings together for the most part only the more devout. At best, sometimes, there is a vague feeling that what passes for a church is not after all a church, because, whilst common prayer is maintained, and the Christian traditions are kept alive, and the household are more or less visited by the pastor, there is no active Christian organism. Acting upon this vague feeling, fellow listeners, fellow worshippers, fellow pew-hirers or pew-owners, being strangers to each other, say suddenly, " Let us be strangers no longer: let us come together; let us be sociable;" and they resolve themselves into a tea party, a talking party, a debating society, sometimes even a dancing party. But, though eating and drinking are sacramental, and to be done unto His glory who came eating and drinking, and exemplifies the religion of every-day life, the case is hardly met. We have houses and assembly rooms for these illustrations of the Master's spirit, and for revealing the divine capabilities of earth and time. Christianity cannot by such means complete itself in a Christian civilization. Though there were no stated preacher or celebrant, the congregation should still gather, drawn together in the spirit of Jesus, — men and women, old and young, taught and untaught, not theologians or ecclesiastics, or delegates to a church convention or congress, but the Christian people, in simple, hearty loyalty to Jesus, with the open Bible in their hands, and hearts set upon righteousness. As towns-people gather together as towns-people, and organize and confer and act in what we call a town meeting, so Christian people should come together in the name of Jesus, and organize as Christian people to carry forward the work of the kingdom of God. There are principles and affections, motives of hope and fear, rulings and precedents, enthusiasms, aspirations, disciplines, which are proper to man as a child of God; and through these He who knows what is in man, and what man needs, binds us into households of faith, hope, and love. In such households, we are engaged to pursue a higher life on earth as under opened heavens; and, so gathered and inspired, we can be no longer pessimists, but only optimists, as they the root of whose being is a divine sonship must needs be. A congregation so gathered and bound in the Spirit can hardly be what the Church so often has been, — "a den of thieves." The State and the Church may seem almost identical, and in simple communities may almost be so; the good townsman scarcely to be distinguished from the good churchman. But, for the most part, Church and State must be two: the one more economical than spiritual and moral, the other more spiritual and moral than economical; and the Church ever proclaiming for the world its higher and more absolute law. I anticipate what will be said about fanaticisms, idiosyncrasies, narrowness, one-sidedness, the ignorance or the insolence of bigotry, the license which makes free with the truth and calls itself liberality; but I fail to see how Jesus encounters any more serious difficulties, as he seeks to gather us now into the light of life and into the path of a practical Christianity, than he met and surmounted in the church at Jerusalem, struggling out of the shadows and forms of the old covenant, or in the church at Corinth, with psalm-singing, prophesying, and speaking with tongues enough to drive a sober, modern church-goer frantic. The churches of Jerusalem, Alexandria, Antioch, and Rome, as that nineteenth article tells us, "have erred, not only in their living and manner of ceremonies, but also in matters of faith;" and this, though they have had much benefit of clergy, and have listened to the tongue of the learned, — for churches, though inspired, are not infallible: they must still be learning more of the truth, and, like the Church of Scotland in our day, rewriting their confessions, and so growing, as the Lord himself grew in wisdom and in stature, and in favor with God and man. And, indeed, the principles and aims of Christianity are so practical, that the wayfaring and unlearned, if only the filial spirit be in him, shall not eer therein. If what we want is light to walk in and to work by, we shall find it, and come together in it, that we may see it lighting up the faces of fellow Christians; and that each man's thought may be confirmed a hundred-fold, when he finds that it is shared by another, and all be patient and hopeful and brave together.

Because of the work which it can do in our world, I long for a revival of the congregation of Christ's flock. I pray that it may accept anew from the Master's own hands his gospel of light and love; that it may be the salt of the earth and a city set on a hill. Christianity must continually begin afresh in the congregation of faithful men and women. No matter how much we may multiply congresses, conventions, convocations, conferences, synods, unless the gospel lives in the congregation, and lives abundantly, its faiths every day made perfect in works, our Christianity is dying. In the congregation as in the germ cell, the mystery of the new creation is enfolded, the promise and the potency of the new heavens and the new earth. And it is especially and profoundly interesting to see what wealth of practical Christian truth is committed to the congregation of the faithful to be transmuted into life; how every jot and tittle of it waits to be applied to our modern societies, to be wrought into their civilization, a savor of life, a principle of divine order, growth, and beauty, destined not merely to relieve superficially and for the moment, but even to anticipate and prevent and stamp out the most threatening ills of the commonwealth and nation.

There are plain Christian principles which bear directly upon human society as we see it to-day, and of which this human society stands in direct need; and it would seem as if the very stones would cry out against us, if we did not come together to set them forth and apply them. These principles are the beginning and the end, the undoubted sum and substance of practical

Christianity, in its relations to a world which it comes to redeem and refashion and beautify. The congregation, like the gatherings of the people for political reform and reconstruction, has its platform, its truths to be transmuted into life, its mind and heart of the meeting, its points to carry, its specific measures to propose, its committees of conference and action. It has something in hand besides the choice and maintenance of a minister, the care of a building, the assessment and collection of taxes, the management of a church sociable. It is a branch of the society which Jesus gathered; it is met before God as he is revealed in Jesus; it holds in its bosom the germ of a life which even yet is not fully expanded; it ought to have counsel and comfort for man in all great straits; it ought to be a power in our age, as in the ages which have gone before it. It would seem that the congregation could hardly lack for topics and interests, if only wise and simple would meet together in the name of Jesus, and set about applying his teachings. His words are as tracts for the times, and need only to be translated out of the language of his day into the language of our day; and scarcely that, so universal was the Lord's speech. Naturally and inevitably, the

Spirit takes of the things of Christ, and shows them unto us, not necessarily in synods and congresses, but in the gathering of the two and three, it may be with differences of manifestation and varieties of application, but always to the same end. Glance for a moment at these great vital truths, — the treasure of the congregation of the faithful, the laws of a Christian commonwealth, the conditions of success in the Christian race.

1. It is our religion, at once its letter and its spirit, that the nature of man can be unfolded, and his earthly life completed and rounded, and all his needs, whether of wisdom, health, beauty, length of days, — all that is truly good, — supplied only in the spirit and power of righteousness, — the righteousness of which God is the source, and our moral being the abiding witness. This is the first plank in the platform: made of seasoned timber, it never gives. Only as we are faithful to our moral instincts, is there any progress of society. The kingdom of God must come first. Without righteousness, nothing; with righteousness, every thing.

2. Again, it is our religion, at once its letter and its spirit, that every thing merely personal and selfish goes into the outer darkness; that

a life centred upon self starves and dies; that the way to get every thing is to give every thing; that what you keep you lose; that what you give you have; that the self which rules out whatsoever is honest, lovely, and of good report, pronounces its own sentence, digs its own grave, and, when it is buried out of sight, the world loses nothing which is worth mentioning.

3. Again, it is our religion, at once its letter and its spirit, that the true human society on earth, under whatsoever form of government, whether Herod reigns or Tiberius, whether the ruler is born or chosen, is that in which each lives for all, and all for each; and the head cannot say to the hand, "I do all the devising, and have no need of thee;" and the hand cannot say to the head, "I do all the labor, and have no need of thee." We are one body in Christ. If we will not rise together as a family and grow together as a vine, if all will be masters and none servants, if we demand not only equality of opportunity, but equality of harvest, then it is vain to talk of prosperity. According to our religion, men must learn to dig and plant and weave and buy and sell for others, just as for ages they have gone to battle and been killed for others. Jesus teaches that, where this is done in love, the life

of the individual, instead of being merged and so lost in the common life, is made more truly individual, real, personal, and precisely and characteristically what God, who has a purpose concerning each one of us, meant it to be; and the result is not a communism, but a commonwealth.

4. And it is our religion, at once its letter and its spirit, that, for motive power, for impulse and restraint, for building men up and holding them to the hard and unceasing labors of life, for securing needful changes in the order of society and inrooted habits of evil, our chief reliance must be upon the inward and spiritual, what comes from within and from above, the good which overcomes evil, the love which casts out fear, believing all things and creat'ng the world it would have, so that the things which are seen are not made of things which appear. Jesus will allow you to make the nation's laws, if you will allow him, in the spirit of his Father, to move upon the nation's heart. His spirit is the spirit of fulfilment, not of destruction. It changes darkness into day simply by being light, and shining into the darkness. It is what it believes in, and believes in it because it is what it believes. So Jesus stands at the door — nay, he is the door — of the kingdom of God on earth,

the vision of prophets, the dream of philosophers, poets, and economists; and teaches, Except ye be converted, born from above, renewed in the spirit of your mind a divine man, you cannot so much as truly see this kingdom, much less enter into it; and, save as such divine men abound, no new heavens and new earths are possible. It was, at least, a true instinct, when the fathers of some of our commonwealths said to those who would join the State, "You must join the Church first." We cannot undertake to carry on human society, save in the fear and love of God. We will have a church, and the rest will follow.

5. And, finally, it is our religion, at once its letter and its spirit, that the kingdom of God is at hand; that to him who believes all things are possible; that the materials from which the kingdom is to be fashioned are within and around; that the King is here, judging the nations, and conspicuously those that have come into the light of his life on earth. The business of Christians is first of all with this world; and they are under an instant necessity to make it Christian, simply because Christianity is the law of its life, — a law as fatal in its working as the law of gravity. Just as when Jesus foretold the swiftly advancing doom of the city so dear to him, so his

spirit speaketh expressly here and now; and whoso readeth, let him understand; whoso hath ears to hear, let him hear, — not of some scarcely conceivable day of judgment in some other and remote world, but of desolations which threaten us and ours. Our worst ills come of our want of confidence in Christianity as the best reason of State, our persistent disregard of its precepts as unpractical, our virtual declaration that we have but one king, who is Cæsar; for whether it be the Jerusalem that fell under the hand of Titus, or these modern cities with their eager crowds, other foundation for earth and time can no man lay than Jesus laid in that answer to Pilate's question, "Art thou a king, then?" — "You have said it." The Lord of life and death, he has opened the heavens for us, that we may work in the light; but this light shines to guide us in our earthly ways. "Behold! I come quickly," is the word of the Lord to each successive age; and his word is continually fulfilled, as many a proud State has learned to its sorrow, and after the things which concerned its peace had been hidden from their eyes.

All this at which I have but hinted is only a part of our wealth as disciples of Jesus. Happily, it is what we are all agreed about, and what concerns our living and working in this present mansion of the Father's house. It is enough to begin with, and as a preparation for that church of the future which can only come out of the church of to-day.

And now the question is asked, "What specially would you have us do?" When the prayers have been prayed, the psalms sung, the sermon preached, the supper ended, what remains? Nothing, it may be, in that hour, except with kindly greetings to part in peace; but the congregation must come together again, and in some place in which they can see eye to eye, and speak brother to brother, and be in very deed a household. Two things they will propose to themselves: to have a distinctively Christian life, and to make this life helpful to others; to be a living church, and, what perhaps is but another name for the same thing, — certainly another expression of the same life, — to be a missionary church.

A church is nourishing its own life when it is adding knowledge and manliness to its faith, by frank and earnest conference bringing it into the light of the present day, and accepting the fresh interpretation of human experience and the world's history, and what we call the logic of events. Christianity is not only what Jesus can teach, but what we can hear; and we must meet together, not as theologians and ecclesiastics meet, but as the people meet, if we would catch the words which alone can save our souls and our State. And the congregation wants for its edification something more than the platitudes of the conference room, however sincerely uttered. We are called upon to love God with all our mind and with all our strength, as well as with all our heart; and, like the apostle Paul, we are to use great plainness of speech. And within the congregation there is a kind of ministering of the strong to the weak, by which the weak are not made weaker, but stronger. The church should strive to present to the world around the image of a community rooted and grounded in a wise love, the good which alone overcomes evil. If the church has its poor, they ought not to be left to the world's charities; and, if any are overtaken in a fault, they should be restored in a tender spirit, and yet with a firm hand. These are hard things, and some will say impossible; but the congregation is met together in the name of Jesus, a society divine beyond any other, encouraged to undertake what for men is impossible, nothing unless it can do what other societies cannot do,—indeed, inferior to our fellowships and lodges and brotherhoods of one sort and another, if the faithful are gathered in a union which is only symbolic, and has no life which it lives in God by the grace of Jesus Christ. That we are fellow Christians of the same Christian household ought to be to us, even in the complications of our modern life, a reality of infinite moment.

And the congregation of the faithful, which is the church of the living God, should have ever upon its mind and heart the pressing needs of those who are near enough to be helped, and not too far away to be pitied. By its very essence, it is missionary, engaged to make converts, under a necessity to preach the gospel; to send forth everywhere its two and two, to meet the ever-pressing demand for personal ministrations amongst the poor, the ignorant, and the vicious; to send brothers of mercy and sisters of charity to prisons; to rescue neglected children from streets and gutters, and establish them in Christian homes; to fill and empty and refill its poor's-purse; to undertake all out-of-door relief of the destitute; to dry up the sources of pauperism and crime; to show how sincerely it desires that the world should be made better by making it better.

Mr. Huxley tells us that any man can do this effectually who is possessed of only two beliefs: the first, that the order of nature is ascertainable by our faculties to an extent which is practically unlimited; the second, that our volition counts for something as a condition of the course of events. Each of these beliefs can be verified experimentally as often as we like to try. Now, if the Church can add to these beliefs the belief of beliefs, — that, if we draw nigh to God, he will draw nigh to us, and help us to make his world better; and if, by awakening in us the knowledge that we are the children of Him who makes the world, it can move us to a deep and tender concern about its awful miseries, — our religion will be seen to be a power, and will scarcely need defenders. It has been well said that, "so long as a Bossuet, a Fénelon, an Arnauld, were alive, the sceptic Bayle made few proselytes. The elevation of Cardinal Dubois and the like immoral priests multiplied unbelievers and indifferents." When the salt has lost its savor, and is salt no longer, it must needs be trampled under the foot of men. And the Church must not limit its ministrations to the work of relieving the poor, much less must it convert its chapels into soup-stations and storehouses of shoes and

THE SOCIETY WHICH JESUS GATHERED. 153

flannel. Its business is to *consider* the weak, and to justify its rooted conviction that no doctrines of the right of the strongest, and the survival of the fittest, and the struggle of life, can supplant and discredit the work and labor of love. Doubtless, it is more blessed to give than to receive; but what so blesses the giver does not, if it is wisely given, harm the receiver. It is the mission of the congregation to illustrate and establish by abundant experience this great Christian truth.

The Church remains. It would remain, though much which passes under its name should perish, and new Catholicism and old Catholicism disappear together, and the spiritual authority of the Pope go the way of all the earth, as the temporal authority seems to have gone, and even priests, presbyters, and preachers vanish in like manner. The two or three shall meet together in the name of Jesus; and *ubi duo aut tres, ibi Ecclesia*, — where are the two or three, there is a church. But the things which remain always need to be strengthened, — if in the beginning, and whilst the heavens were all ablaze with the brightness of the just vanished form of the Lord, why not in these last days and in these ends of the earth? Things are strong only as we are strong in them: not in the air, but in the lives of men, and specially in men who are met together and are one body, in which the Spirit may be for ever incarnate, and no disembodied ghost, — in the world, though not of the world, transmuting and transfiguring and recreating unto the measure of the stature of the fulness of Christ.

VII.

THE LIFE ETERNAL.—HEAVEN AND HELL.

BY REV. SAMUEL R. CALTHROP.

THERE are two great affirmations which the writers of the Bible are continually making: first, the unchangeable, eternal love of God,— and this without any limitation or drawback whatever; secondly, the unchangeable, eternal law of retribution,— and this, too, without limitation or drawback. They do this without attempting any reconciliation between the two, — rather, perhaps, without a thought that the two needed reconciliation. The Christian Church has made an age-long attempt to reconcile these two. The Orthodox believer has generally attempted to do this by belittling the first,— the eternal love; the Liberal, by belittling the last, — the eternal retribution.

Until very lately, both sides carried on the contest with theological weapons, and on high, *a priori* grounds. Neither side sufficiently investigated the facts of things,— resolutely endeavored to trace out the actual workings of the laws of the universe here and now, which here and now are working in the same way in which they have worked and will work for ever and ever. This earth floats now in the midst of the one Infinity. There is only one universe, and we are now inside it; only one law, and we now governed by it. Why not, then, here and now endeavor to find out what law it is that thus surrounds us?

Says Alison. "The sins of individuals are not always punished in this world. But nations have no immortality; and therefore" God has to punish them in this world. There is a mixture of truth and error here. It is as if he said, "As nations have no immortality, God is obliged to alter his laws of retribution to meet their case, as otherwise they would go scot free." But God's laws of retribution move on unchanging ever, slackening not to save, nor hastening to punish. The truth is, that not always, in the small space of individual life, has the orb of divine retribution time to come round full circle; whereas, in the life of a nation, with its millennial periods, it has time for one or more full revolutions.

The earth has been in existence at least a

hundred million years, life has been on it at least ten million, man has been on it at least ten thousand. In any case, we have a very large time arc with which to calculate the sweep and orbit of the eternal laws.

When once we look directly at the facts around us, we can see that a single fact is sufficient to prove that, taking for granted that the law is the same for ever and ever, the average Orthodox reconciler is in error. No man has hitherto been produced, in whose character absolutely nothing but evil has been proved to exist; and, certainly, no body of men has ever been got together, and been proved to be absolutely incapable of being influenced toward the better. Take the scum of all England, and dump them down in a wretched Norfolk Island, and you can soon establish a pandemonium. But if a Captain Machonochie come there too, with the cross of Christ in his hand and the blood of Christ in his heart, then the hell-fires forthwith begin to pale, and God's stars begin to shine out again on the poor, forlorn, human lives below.

A single fact will also tend to show that the average Liberal reconciler has been no nearer the truth. No man has hitherto been found in whose case retribution has ceased to act, simply because retribution has ceased to do him good. No drunkard has yet been produced on whom whiskey has ceased to exercise an intoxicating influence, simply because a merciful God has seen that it is of no use to expect that the man will stop drinking on account of the retribution attending it. Hitherto, the universal experience has been that the more the man drinks, the worse he gets, and the more is he punished. Hitherto, the only way to stop retribution in the drunkard's case is to persuade him to stop drinking.

The only thorough reconcilement will come when we see that heaven and hell are alike the results of the workings of one and the self-same law. "The laws of disease are as beautiful as the laws of health," say the physicians. I assert that the laws of disease are the laws of health. The same law working one way produces health; working the other, disease. So heaven and hell are each but special illustrations of the one and the same law of consequences.

This law is already enthroned in our conception of nature. It is the basis of all science. Ere long, it will be seen to be the basis of the soul's world also. *Heaven* is that special result of the law of consequences whereby good causes produce good consequences. Heaven is eternal, because the law that makes it is eternal. Eternally, good causes produce good consequences. A good tree cannot have evil fruit. *Hell* is that special result of the law of consequences, whereby evil causes produce evil consequences. Hell is eternal, because the law that makes it is eternal. Eternally, evil causes produce evil consequences. An evil tree cannot have good fruit. The Buddhists have a doctrine which they call Karma. It is the doctrine of consequences. Your life is a wheel with a million spokes, each spoke an act, a thought, a word. In that life-wheel of yours you have placed a thousand thousand white spokes, with only here and there a black one. In the inevitable revolution, each white spoke in its turn comes uppermost, and will bring you to the heaven corresponding to the good deed it represents. There you taste its special joys, while the wheel keeps slowly, slowly turning. But it moves, nevertheless; and then another spoke takes the place of the first. Is it white, then you pass from joy to joy, — from a known bliss to an unknown; but is it black, then it forces you down, down to the hell corresponding to the evil deed that carved that black spoke, there to abide during the long ages in which that black spoke is uppermost upon the slowly turning wheel. At last, at last, another spoke comes uppermost; and, if that spoke is white, then you are emancipated once more, while the awful wheel keeps slowly turning. It is an allegory, you say. Take, then, to heart the truth it contains.

1. Heaven is good cause, — good consequence. It is the prerogative of inspired genius to anticipate, sometimes by centuries, the slow conclusions of the understanding. Evolution was reached but yesterday. But Jesus sees that the law of life is growth. The kingdom of heaven is leaven, is seed, is the growing corn; first the blade, then the ear, then the full corn in the ear. The reign of law is a nineteenth century conception. But all the great sayings of Jesus are based upon the law of consequences. The Beatitudes are each a separate illustration of this. The blessing grows out of the vital condition. Virtue is rewarded by growth, by more virtue. Blessed are the pure: they shall see the all-pure. Blessed are they that hunger and thirst after righteousness; for they shall be filled with righteousness. Blessed are the pitiful; for on them the pity eternal shall descend. Forgive, and ye shall be forgiven; give, it shall be given

to you; show kindness, kindness shall be shown to you; ask, and ye shall receive; seek, and ye shall find; knock, and it shall be opened to you; do good, that ye may be the children of the All-Good; love your enemies, that ye may be the children of Him who loves His enemies. On the other hand, Judge not, that ye be not judged; condemn not, that ye be not condemned. With what measure ye mete, *in* that self-same measure it shall be measured to you again. If ye forgive not, ye shall not be forgiven.

According to Jesus, then, the rewards of heaven grow out of the very life and essence of the nobleness rewarded. Innocence clothes herself in white, as does the lily, by simply growing. " The garments of the angels," says Swedenborg, "grow mysteriously out of the emanations of their own characters."

2. Hell is evil cause,—evil consequence. It is " curses, like chickens, coming home to roost." He loved cursing, so cursing shall come to him; he hated blessing, so it shall be far from him. Be not deceived: God is not mocked. That which a man sowed, that shall he also reap. He sowed the wind: he reaped the whirlwind. This law is eternal: therefore hell is eternal. There never was a time when it existed not; there never

will be a time when it shall cease to be. It is also omnipresent. It is on the earth, and in every star, and in the spaces between the stars. It is in this world: it is in the next. Speaking theologically, as God's thought of goodness, harmony, and love eternally produces heaven, so God's thought of sin, discord, and hate eternally produces hell. How long, then, will hell exist? Potentially, as long as God exists; that is, it will eternally manifest itself under certain conditions.

Consider one moment. Is it not absurd to suppose that God's judgment about a mean, selfish, cowardly, treacherous, cruel, or malignant act can ever change? Will there ever come a time in the years of heaven when meanness shall cease to be mean in God's sight? when to him, for very pity, a lie shall seem to be truthful, hate lovely, and oppression just? Nay, more. Can you even imagine that your own private opinion of such things can ever change? You cannot, and why? Because you inherit into the eternal mind.

Where is hell? Potentially, wherever God is; that is, that under certain conditions God's presence creates hell, as under certain other conditions God's presence creates heaven. God is everywhere. There is no inch of space from which his truth, his justice, his love, are absent; in which, if they are received and welcomed, they will not bless; in which, if they are rejected and set at naught, they will not punish. Nowhere does hate bring happiness; nowhere does self-seeking satisfy, wrong triumph, or falsehood bless. Hell, then, is potentially everywhere; that is, it will manifest itself wherever wrong, sin, discord, selfishness, exist; will begin to show itself precisely at the same moment that they show themselves. Does any one doubt this? Let him go home, and there, in the dark, obey the fundamental law of hell, which is frantic self-seeking, and see if it do not start up at once from underneath the floor. There is no surer instinct in the heart of man than his prophetic sense that punishment eternally follows wrong. Whenever gross wrong is committed, whenever the weak are oppressed, whenever the fatherless and widow are robbed of their inheritance, whenever crime brings seeming success, — no matter how high the offender, how surrounded with whole armies of guards, or how low and weak and unaided the souls he tramples on, — the indignant, outraged heart of man is sure, as if God spoke it from heaven, that a day of reckoning will come, that innocent blood will be avenged. All is well; for, if any thing is not well, it is well that it should not be well. It is well that oppression should not be well; that envy, hatred, malice, and all uncharitableness should not be well. If these things were well, — if human happiness came from them, — then God were no God at all, but an omnipotent devil, the laws of whose world worked for the bad against the good, for darkness against light. The presence of God, the immanence of God, is as much proved by the existence of hell as by the existence of heaven.

It is in vain to hope that hell is confined to this life and this earth. God knows we have enough of it here; but a careful study of its phenomena here is enough to teach us that it stretches far on into the hereafter.

There was once, at an English university, an able man of peculiarly fascinating manners and magnetic influence on all who came near him, — an influence which he too often used for purely selfish ends. He was a thorough man of pleasure, and seemed utterly careless of the misery or remorse which his gratification brought to others. This man was suddenly stricken down with a seemingly fatal disease, — a disease, however, which left his head clear to think. In the long, weary hours of day and night, thoughts, which in health he had forced away, began to crowd upon his soul. What a pitiful, mean, contemptible life his had been! How utterly purposeless, how small, how unworthy of his powers, — powers which had so often caused only misery, when they might have brought blessing! At last, the eternal judgment on such as he arose in his mind clear and strong; and from his burdened heart he put up a prayer for life, — not from any mean fear of death, but simply that he might have time to undo the dreadful evil he had done. The prayer seemed granted. He rose to life and health again, and at once prepared to fulfil the sacred promise he had made. Of all his past sins, the meanest and blackest seemed to be one that he had committed against a simple, innocent, and loving soul that had fatally trusted him. He resolved to search for that poor, lost woman, — lost through him. But such lost ones are often hard to find. He went to live in London, and devoted himself to the lifting up of such as he feared she had become; and many that had been dead arose and called him blessed. But, day after day and night after night, his search after that one continued. At last, one dark midnight, he was standing watching by a lamp-post the stream of painted misery as it swept by him on the pavement: the door of an evil house close by burst open, and two drunken women, fighting, scratching, tearing each other, staggered out. One gave the other a violent blow, which felled her, and caused her head to strike against the curbstone. It was over in a moment. The watcher sprang forward, and bent down to help the fallen woman. Tenderly he took off her poor, torn bonnet, and then by the lamplight he gazed at the poor dead face; for he saw at once that the blow had killed her. He gazed, and out from that sordid misery came the ghastly likeness of the face he had so long sought in vain. Then he found that, in one short earth-life, there was not time enough to undo the evil he had done. And, therefore, he prayed once again that God might mercifully teach him to scorn the thought of rest in heaven, till that poor, lost soul, cleansed from every stain, should enter with him the blessed gates. The vision is for many days.

The Irish girl devoutly believes that she can help to pray her parents out of purgatory. And so she can, if she prays the right kind of prayer. Get rid, my friend, of every vulgar taint that father or mother put into your blood. That is the help they sorely need from you. What self-respecting parent can dare to think of heaven for himself, while low propensities of his own planting are alive in the breast of his son,— ay, or his son's son? It is said that there are noble families in England suffering still from the consequences of the pleasures of the reign of Charles the Second. How much heaven can the pleasure-loving ancestor enjoy, think you, though he repented never so sincerely at the eleventh hour, while seed of his sowing is still ripening to bitter fruit? The vision is for many days.

This is a terrible statement, you say. Yes, terrible, but true; and it needs the most powerful statement of its terror and its truth to rouse up the miserable sleepers in our own too comfortable Zion. A man tells you, with much unction: "Oh, yes! I believe in universal salvation. I argue it with all my friends!" and forthwith expects you to welcome him with open arms as a brother, while it is very probably your duty to say to him: "Sir, I am heartily sorry to hear you say this. Just such do-nothings and be-nothings as you are the leaden weights which are sinking our holy cause. It is such as you that make the free gospel of the love eternal contemptible. The one boon you can confer upon us, while your life continues to be as mean and vulgar as it is, is to cease, if only for our sakes, to believe it."

The saddest thing is that some really fine spirits are to-day in some such prison as this. "Great grief seized me," says Dante, "for I knew that great souls were in that limbo." The most tragi-comic of all the hells is the hell whither those go who do not believe there is any hell.

When the mighty Theseus sought a bride for his friend, Pirithous, he resolved to descend to Hades, and thence abduct the fair Proserpine herself, the one flower of Pluto's dreary realm. He descended: he passed without attack the great three-headed dog of hell; the Furies' snakes hissed not at him; the fires of Tartarus themselves seemed to fear to touch so great a hero as he. No one dared molest him; so, after wandering awhile till he was weary, he sat down on a great stone to rest himself. Till that moment, he himself had not even guessed how great a man he was. What lordly power must sit on his brow, that hell itself should fear him! He sat and sat, in full-browed contemplation. At last, quite rested, he resolved to arise and resume his journey; but he found that he could not get up. Only this, and nothing more. No torture, no Furies' scourges, no fire, no devouring beast. He merely was unable to get up or do any thing but sit; and the story leaves him there. Theseus sits, and for ever will sit. Such vengeance did the irony of the gods inflict on him.

I have seen admirable, heroic Liberals sitting in this very hell. And the tragedy is that they will never know it till, like Theseus, they try to get up. They sit; and human life, with all its wild sorrow, its unsatisfied longing, its unanswered questions, passes by them in sad procession; but still there they sit. They sit and wait; and justice also waits, truth waits, love waits, heaven waits, and hell enlarges its borders, and cries out, "There is room!"

3. But, these things being so, what hope is there, or can there be, for mankind as a whole? The first hope for mankind is based on the fact that hell is eternal; for, the moment it ceased to be so, that moment it would hopelessly begin. It is the persistency of God in the natural world, where every natural cause is indissolubly linked to its consequence, which alone enables man to learn the laws which govern matter, and lovingly to obey them. And it is the persistency of God

in the spiritual world, where every spiritual cause is indissolubly linked to its consequence, which alone enables man to learn the laws of spirit, and lovingly to obey them.

If fire burned to-day, and did not burn to-morrow, no child would have any fingers left. Just because fire eternally burns, the stupidest child learns at last not to put his fingers into it. Certain chemical combinations are always possible, and, when made, the result is eternally the same; but that is no reason why we need make the combinations. Here is a white-hot poker, yonder is a barrel of gunpowder. Certain very surprising results eternally ensue, if I plunge that poker into that gunpowder; but that is the very reason why I do not plunge that poker into that gunpowder. Just so, if sin harmed to-day and did not harm to-morrow, how could we know the eternal connection between sin and sorrow? Just because the fires of hate eternally burn, the most foolish of us can learn at last not to hate; just because for ever crime stabs itself with its own hands, men will at last learn not to commit crime. Envy, malice, and uncharitableness eternally poison the soul's life; but that will not harm us, when we have learned not to be envious, malicious, uncharitable. Ignorance will always err; but that fact will not harm us, when knowledge has become pleasant to our souls. Hate will always make life hateful; but that will not harm us, when Christ's own love is shed abroad in our hearts.

We look for God's mercy in the wrong place. We foolishly think that we shall find it in his reluctance to inflict pain, or certainly in his refusal to keep on inflicting pain after a certain limited time; whereas it is just that pain, that anguish, that gnashing of teeth, which is the dread but loving angel of his presence, — which sternly yet most mercifully refuses to allow one atom of hate to bring happiness, one atom of cursing to bring blessing, through all the eternal years.

The second hope rests in the fact that heaven is eternal. The gates of heaven are eternally open. Whosoever wills can enter in for ever and ever. And the gates of heaven are everywhere. "Hell is not two hand-breadths from heaven." You can pass from one to the other by one single leap of the will. If God loved men to-day, and did not love them to-morrow, — loved them in this life, and did not love them in the next, — then mankind would sink in despair. But, just because God loves mankind eternally, the most foolish of men will find out God's love at last. It waits and waits, till the blindest soul shall see it. Yes, here is the hope. Ever let us remember that we all, saint and sinner alike, are living, and will for ever live, in the midst of God, bathed for ever by the waves of that unutterable deep of love, that hath no shore.

The third and last hope is the gospel. That is the good tidings of the love eternal entering the heart of man, and from that essential vantage-ground working on man's destiny. It is God incarnate in man. The gospel message is that God is eternally God; Christ, Christ; and good men, good men. If the gospel said, "Be good to-day, so that you need not be good to-morrow," "Love all mankind in this world, so that you need not do so any more in the next," then there would be no hope that man would ever perform his essential part in the work of human redemption; that the good tidings would ever get preached to the spirits in prison; that, upon those who now sit in darkness and the shadow of death, the true light would ever shine. But it is just because the gospel is eternally the same, just because goodness is for ever true to itself, — for ever manifests its gracious quality as helper and redeemer of lost souls everywhere,

— that we are able to cling to the eternal hope.

This is a point which any manly mind can see, my friend. You may have been confused by the Babel voices of creed and dogma. You may not as yet know that God is infinitely good, and therefore infinitely adorable, though for that knowledge you may have searched as for hid treasure. But this at least you can see, — that it is a manly attitude for you to take, to resolve to stand by mankind, whatever comes of it; to share the fate of man, whatever that fate may be. And you can see also that it is a cowardly attitude for you to take, to be ready and willing to accept a heaven in which your forlorn brothers and sisters have no share. Act, then, on this golden gleam of insight, and already half the gospel is your own; for you have resolved to love your neighbor as yourself. This third hope is as essential as the love of God himself. Man is eternally bound to man. Man's redemption is worked out by God working in man, by man, through man. In all reverence, then, we say that it is impossible for God to save mankind without man's help, — without God's being present, not only outside of, but inside of, human consciousness. It is the doctrine of the incarnation. If, then, we wait for God outside of man to do what only God and man acting together can do, we may wait for ever, and wait in vain. God has no hands. It is therefore folly to pray that he will do what only hands can do. When God needs hands, he creates them, and puts a keen brain above them and a loving heart abreast of them, and bids them do his beautiful will. God, then, strikes a wrong through a true man's hands. If the true man folds his arms up, then the proud, boastful wrong stalks unsmitten and defiant. There is such a brutal directness in the force of wrong that we are prone, in our atheism, to believe that, in a certain way, it is stronger than right. And so it is, in a certain way. A fierce, proud, self-confident wrong is stronger than a timid, apologizing, mistrustful right. A milk-and-water angel is no match for a masterful devil. Only when Michael, the strong archangel, God's valiant knight, sworn defender of his oppressed and despised truth and love, fights against Satan, then, and then only, is that old serpent sure to bite the dust.

Friends, we have this matter in our own hands. Under God, the human will is the final arbiter of this mighty question. Hell for man will last just as long as man chooses it to last. How long will the hell in Washington or New York last? Just as long as the men and women of New York or Washington please. Let us, then, cease to ask, " Is hell eternal?" Thank God it is, in the sense that eternally evil causes produce evil effects. Let us rather ask, " How long, friends and lovers and servants of the eternal love, shall we suffer this and that human hell to last? In the name of the Eternal, let us rise up and cause it to cease." Hell fears such words as these, and vanishes everywhere before the deeds they prompt.

Who loves man as God loves him, for ever and ever? Who has cast behind his back, with manly scorn, all dream of a selfish bliss, — of a bliss which all mankind everywhere, in this world and in the next, do not share? Who has resolved to share the fate of man, come weal, come woe, heaven or no heaven? God waits for us to take this attitude, that he may give us his full blessing, which is the fulness of his spirit, which is himself. " He that loveth his soul shall lose it; but he that loseth his soul for God's sake, for man's sake, shall find it."

Featured Titles from Westphalia Press

Peasant Art in Sweden, Lapland and Iceland
by Charles Holme

This particular work offers a carefully chosen selection of both the decorative and fine arts of Sweden, Iceland, and the northern most region of Finland. A comprehensive survey, it includes paintings, jewelry, textiles, metalwork, carving, furniture and pottery.

The Rise of the Book Plate: An Exemplative of the Art
by W. G. Bowdoin, Introduction by Henry Blackwel

Bookplates were made to denote ownership and hopefully steer the volume back to the rightful shelf if borrowed. They often contained highly stylized writing, drawings, coat of arms, badges or other images of interest to the owner.

The Art of Table Setting, Ancient and Modern
by Claudia Quigley Murphy

The arrangement of a table in terms of cutlery, arrangement, serving style, and timing of courses has changed a great deal over time and now is enjoying renewed interest. The History of the Art of Tablesetting was written by a true expert in the field, Claudia Quigley Murphy.

Understanding Art: Hendrik Willem Van Loon's
How To Look At Pictures by Hendrik Willem Van
Loon, Introduction by Daniel Gutierrez-Sandoval

Hendrik Willem van Loon was a Dutch-American professor, journalist, prolific writer, and illustrator. His most famous work, "The Story of Mankind" earned him the prestigious John Newbery Medal.

The Etchings of Rembrandt: A Study and History
by P. G. Hamerton

Philip Gilbert Hamerton (1834-1894) was an Englishman who was devoted to the arts in numerous forms. Due to the praise, Hamerton stuck with art criticism, and went on to write other works. He also wrote novels, biographies, and reflections on society.

Lankes, His Woodcut Bookplates by Wilbur Macey Stone

Julius John Lankes was born in Buffalo, New York in 1884, and became a prolific woodcut print artist, as well as an author and professor. As a child, he enjoyed working with the scraps of wood his father brought home from the lumber mill where he was employed. Lankes had a lifelong interest in art.

Los Dibujos de Heriberto Juarez / The Drawings of Heriberto Juarez, Edited by Paul Rich

That the drawings here are from life in México is not surprising because Juárez is constantly, and at times impishly, putting art into life and getting art from life. He doesn't think of art as some thing that is done just in a studio or for that matter kept in museums and looked at on Sundays.

The History of Photography: Carl W. Ackerman's George Eastman by Carl W. Ackerman, Introduction by Daniel Gutierrez-Sandoval

The life of George Eastman is very much a part of the history of contemporary photography. Founder of the Eastman Kodak Company, Eastman was an enthusiastic photographer himself who became instrumental in bringing photography to the mainstream.

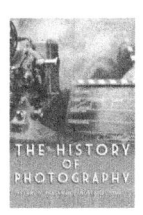

Famous Stars of Light Opera by Lewis C. Strang, Introduction by Matthew Brewer

Strang's attempts to quantify the humorous elements of each performer, as well as quotes from the performers themselves attempting to explain their own success, are an interesting exercise in attempting to explain the inexplicable.

Wood Sculpture: From Ancient Egypt to the End of the Gothic Period by Alfred Maskell F.S.A.

Alfred Maskell was an artist, primarily a photographer, who worked tirelessly to advance the art. Maskell, along with Robert Memachy, helped to develop the gum-bichromate printing, which is able to create a unique painterly image from negatives. This work highlights a variety of wood-based art over time.

westphaliapress.org

Made in the USA
Coppell, TX
11 January 2021